The Elementary

School Library in

ACTION

The Elementary School Library in ACTION

by

Lora Palovic

and

Elizabeth B. Goodman

Parker Publishing Company, Inc.
West Nyack, New York

Third Printing, ... April, 1969

PRINTED IN THE UNITED STATES OF AMERICA

B & P

Dedication

This book is dedicated to
Mrs. Gertrude Stacy
who pioneered the Sunnyvale School District libraries
and to our former principals
Mr. DeLoy Smith
Mr. Donn Wadley.
Without their support and encouragement we could not have
developed the programs upon which this book is based.

Foreword

Every school librarian finds, with experience, that an effective program for school library services can be best developed with thought, imagination, experimentation, flexibility, and much evaluation. There are no short cuts to such a program; knowledge and experience are necessary.

Lora Palovic and Elizabeth Goodman introduce the reader to their interpretation of a school library program. They offer practical information about the librarian's responsibility for each activity. Explanations are presented so the reader can understand why the authors say what they do. At the same time, the many dimensions of a school library program are indicated.

These two dedicated school librarians have drawn from their backgrounds of experience and have selected the ideas and the information that have proved helpful in their work. This is their way of looking, and they offer this to the reader with the hope that the road to more effective school library service will be illuminated.

MAE J. DURHAM

School of Librarianship
University of California, Berkeley

The Purpose and Structure of This Book

Today the desirability of a centralized library in the elementary school is generally recognized by all educators. The results of the Knapp Foundation Grant of $1,300,000 to the American Library Association dramatically demonstrate the validity of this point of view.

National Defense Education Funds have assisted school districts with book purchasing. Public Law 98-10 has made available to school districts millions of dollars for library books and audio-visual materials. These two Federal programs are stimulating the development of school libraries in every state in the union. Additional impetus is provided by the American Library Association's *Standards for School Libraries,* which points out what an ideal library should be and sets goals toward which all librarians need to work.

As school libraries develop and expand, the need for professional librarians, familiar with this specialized field, is evident. But the need has far outstripped the supply, and many people untrained in the field will need to fill the librarian's role—teachers, parents, and others.

It is the purpose of this book to provide guidelines and suggestions to meet the day-to-day needs of these people. It is hoped it will also be useful to professional librarians.

Each chapter treats a phase of library skills from its introduction at the level the child is ready to receive it to its conclusion at a point appropriate for elementary school children. Some schools are able to give such instruction at earlier grade levels than others. Grade levels are mentioned only because the authors' experiences have shown that children can, at that grade level, absorb the particular skill under discussion. It is hoped that the lessons are sufficiently flexible for the librarian to adapt them to the needs of the groups she works with—following the outline as suggested, or telescoping steps, transposing them to other units or grade levels, omitting them as necessary. Each group provides a different problem in learning from every other group. Therefore the librarian involved will need to decide in consultation with the teacher what materials are most appropriate for each class. Neither author, in her own library, carries out all the activities discussed in this book, but all at one time or another have been successfully used.

The program of instruction in a particular basic skill is presented, then, as a whole, chapter by chapter, to allow each group to travel to the fullest extent possible. The authors do not necessarily present the material in the chapter order indicated, e.g., one librarian may wish to teach the Dewey Decimal System *before* the card catalog. The order of the chapters does not reflect the importance of the subject matter.

The novice will need to exercise care to avoid becoming enmeshed in subject material whose proper place is the classroom. She must bear in mind that her focus is application only of *library* skills to any given subject.

The authors are librarians in one of California's forward-looking elementary school districts.[1] No school library in the district yet meets standards for personnel recommended in the *Standards for School Libraries*. However the high quality of library instruction in library skills which is offered from kindergarten through sixth grade, and on which this book is based, would certainly meet these goals.

All incidents which are described or commented on are true, although Willie and Debra are fictional characters. These incidents are part of the daily excitement of running a library in an elementary school, where the unexpected is part of the routine.

THE AUTHORS

Sunnyvale, California

---

[1] Sunnyvale Elementary School District, about 50 miles south of San Francisco.

Acknowledgments

We are most appreciative of the help and criticism given us by the following people:

Mr. Walter W. Fox, Coordinator, Audio-Visual Technical Services, Audio-Visual Service Center, San Jose State College, San Jose, California

Dr. Joseph Goodman, Research Biochemist, Veterans' Administration Hospital, San Francisco, California

Mrs. Ann Rahm, Librarian, Chapman Intermediate School, Garden Grove, California

Miss Lesley Rahm, Librarian, Ampex Corporation, Los Angeles, California

Miss Lois Ralston, English Language Consultant for the Junior/Senior High Schools, Okayama, Japan; formerly District Librarian, Sunnyvale Elementary School District, Sunnyvale, California

Sunnyvale, California, Elementary School District Personnel:
Mrs. Bea Faber, Secretary, San Miguel Elementary School
Mrs. Rose Malone, Librarian, Edwina Benner Intermediate School
Mrs. Margaret Martin, Secretary, Business Department
Mr. Charlie S. Newton, Principal, San Miguel Elementary School
Mr. Roland Smith, Principal, Jarvis E. Bishop Elementary School
Mrs. Gertrude Stacy, Coordinator (retired), Library Services

Drawings in this book are by Lora Palovic and the photography by Frode Jensen, Lora Palovic, and Lue Ann Wright.

Contents

xiii

Contents

Chapter 1—

Building for the Future—

Beginning Activities for

Each Grade

A general overall view of the library picture herein will give the librarian some idea of what this book will cover in detail: the setting, the beginning activities of each grade, from kindergarten through the intermediate grades.

Because the activities of kindergartners, first, and second graders throughout the year are basically story-telling, reviewing books, and checking out books, their initial activities such as the process of checking out a book are described in detail in this first chapter.

The introductions for third grade on are brief since detailed accounts of activities and lessons follow chapter by chapter.

SETTING

Firing the imagination is reason enough to become excited about one's library environment—thus, questions such as "What kind of plant is this? How can it grow so many leaves when it's only in water? Where does it get the food it needs for all the green leaves? Why is it in the library at all?"—these justify a sweet potato in the library from its beginning to its full growth. The librarian lifts out from the transparent jar the plant with its tangled root system and hollow shell. Through inquiry, she stimulates the thinking of the primary children who look and listen in wide-eyed wonder. This is

1

one example of how environment can instill attitudes children develop toward a library.

An orderly and harmonious room, stimulating bulletin boards, and quiet voices create a pleasant mood. (See Figures 1–1, 1–2, and 1–3.) When children forget or become excited and noisy, a librarian waiting silently need offer no better way of achieving silence.

To maintain this pleasant, quiet atmosphere, it is vital for the children to know where freedom ends and responsibility begins. The librarian, as a member of the staff, teaches these principles and encourages them in the children through praising a class where praise is deserved. When the children are on their best behavior (and sometimes only second best) the alert librarian remembers to comment on it. Sixth graders, too, like to hear, "You've been an excellent class today; in fact, you've acted like adults," just as the primaries often hear "My, you walked in as quietly as mice. I didn't even know you were here."

Figure 1–1.

Figure 1–2.

Figure 1–3.

The arrangement of furniture and library materials also contributes to a harmonious environment; e.g., the card catalog is located to the best advantage of the users. The books are logically arranged. The encyclopedias and other references are situated to best meet the physical needs of the children; e.g., these are placed on lower shelves so they need not stretch to see and reach them. An aquarium is set where curious eyes may easily peer through the glass to see the fish. Such an item does not appear on a library blueprint, but it is an essential part of this environment.

These simple devices then—quiet tones, moments of silence, harmonious and pleasing surroundings, judicious praise—develop a peaceful environment that is calming to the spirit of the individual. In such a setting children have the opportunity to enjoy the library, and they have the leisure for natural curiosity to bubble up to the surface, with plenty of books to browse among to fulfill that curiosity.

IN THE BEGINNING

Kindergarten

The kindergartners first view the library on their initial tour of the school. The librarian welcomes them with a smile and a wave of the hand and invites them to return soon for a longer stay.

Step 1—On their first formal visit the children hear about several areas of importance to them. Among these are the sources of their classroom picture books and pictures. The librarian shows them the section of the library where the Easy, or picture, books are shelved from which the children may help select books for the classroom collections. She indicates the vertical file, opening the drawers and holding up to view pictures of ships, machines, etc., which the teacher may check out for use in the classroom.

Step 2—Since handling picture books is part of the daily kindergarten routine, the librarian reinforces the classroom instruction on the proper handling of books:

1. Books are used when hands are clean.
2. Book pages are turned at the fore edges.
3. A book is opened no further than the flat surface of a table so the back will not break.

Marking books with crayons or pencils and cutting pictures is discussed from the point of view of special books for special purposes: color books for coloring, cut-out books for cutting, but picture books to look at and enjoy just as they are. At this time, children are asked not to mend books at home with Scotch tape, but to leave the mending to the librarian. The children learn the reasons for this: Scotch tape turns yellow with age and dirt collects around its edges. The librarian therefore asks the children simply to show her the torn pages so she can mend these before the book circulates again.

A bulletin board display stimulates the children to discuss the reasons for clean hands in handling books, not only in the library, but in the classroom, at home, bookstores—everywhere (Figures 1–4 and 1–5).

This information, followed by a short story, is as much as kindergartners can absorb at one time.

Figure 1–4.

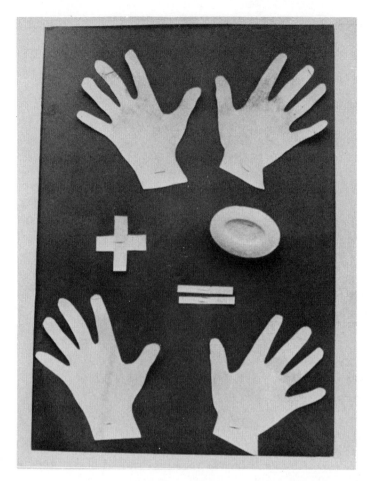

Figure 1–5.

Step 3—When the children enter the library, they sit in their usual area whether it be before the fireplace or other space provided. They review the rules about clean hands and turning pages. Then the librarian asks them to sit at the tables where many books are on display. Do they really know how to turn the pages properly? They get acquainted with the books while demonstrating that they *do* know how to turn the pages.

Throughout the year the children, during their visits, may sit informally in a semi-circle on the floor for story hour. In a small library, sometimes it may be necessary for them to sit at tables. Twenty minutes are about the attention span of kindergartners. They hear the librarian tell one or two stories and they see one or two picture books she shows or reads. At the end of this time, she may compliment them on their excellent attention. Then the teacher may dismiss the children in the way she is accustomed to doing in the classroom.

Grade 1

Step 1—The first graders start with a tour of the library—a little more extended than they had as kindergartners. The librarian points out the circulation desk, the exhibit areas, the magazines for primaries, the fire exit, and the Easy section. Before leaving, the children hear a story from the librarian.

Step 2—Willie and Debra, as first graders, review the reasons for clean hands, and particularly handling books properly. In addition, they discuss

1. How does one mark the place in a book when dinner time comes?
2. What happens when
    a. a pencil is used as a bookmark?
    b. pages are turned from the edges near the bound side?
    c. an open book is turned face down?
    d. a page corner is creased to mark the place?

Many examples of incorrect usage found in the library are held up for the children to see and analyze:

Loose or torn spine
Torn pages at inner edges
Scotch-taped pages
Crayoned or inked book

One example is the undesirable "dog-ear" type of bookmark. The librarian illustrates by turning down the corner of a piece of paper, showing how the fold looks like a puppy's floppy ear. Forever after, the class will remember, "Never dog-ear your books!" (See Figure 1–6.) Before leaving, the children hear another story from the librarian.

Figure 1–6.

Step 3—During the weeks of early library experiences, the children sit at tables lined with picture books. They enjoy the excitement of handling books, showing the librarian and the teacher they know how to turn the pages. They participate conscientiously. The librarian and the teacher note carefully whether they are turning the pages properly. The children feel important, too, because they are also helping the teacher to select books for the library reading corner in the classroom. They enjoy the librarian's stories which may be varied with storytelling records, and filmstrips of favorite stories such as "The Story of Ping." These activities continue throughout the year.

GETTING UNDER WAY

Step 4—Eventually comes one of the biggest moments in a first grader's library experiences: his first time to check out a book (Figures 1–7 and 1–8). But first, the preparation! What does one do to take a book out of the library? By the time February rolls around, a first grader has learned to print both his first and last names. By this time too, with directions from the librarian and with practice in both the library and the classroom where dittoed sample cards are used, the child has learned to print small enough to get his whole name and room number on one line of the card, still leaving enough space for the date to be stamped.[1] He needs to be encouraged in the exercise, although the incentive of checking out a book will bring about the desired result when preparations are started far ahead of time.

No sloppy printing of first names only, skipping lines, or taking two lines for a name! This is the time to set the standard. The average first grader is capable of accomplishing far more than he is given credit for. The few exceptions, who may be like pre-schooler Rufus M., receive help. Printing his name to size and order is a tremendous accomplishment for a first grader since he is accustomed to printing in large letters. And when he does master it, he glows at the well-deserved praise he receives as the librarian stamps his book and compliments his efforts.

---

[1] If kindergartners check out books, they print only their first names and room numbers on the book cards.

Figure 1–7.

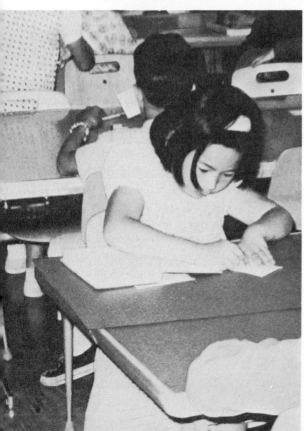

Figure 1–8.

Figure 1–9.

Step 5—The final lesson on checking out a book occurs. A large sample book card on *Blueberries for Sal,* or some other favorite, is outlined on tagboard or on the chalkboard before the class arrives. Directions are once more given or pointed out on how to sign out a book. As illustrated in Figure 1–9, several children in turn go to the board to fill in the "card" properly with the necessary information:

Oct. 3	John Doe	6

The librarian on this special occasion may review books for the children to check out. Enough books are reviewed for each child to make a choice. On other occasions, the librarian may dismiss the children to browse and make selections from the picture books placed on the tables and display counter. Later they choose books from the Easy cubbies or shelves, but on the first few rounds they take the books reviewed and those on display.

When each child has made his selection,[2] he takes it to a table where the teacher is waiting to assist him, or he goes to the librarian at the counter. When he has signed the card properly, he gives the book and card to the librarian to stamp. She gives him a bookmark and praises him on his performance: the choice of book, the proper printing, and neatness.

---

[2] See Appendix for parent approval of children bringing books home from the library.

The child may then be seated—on the floor in libraries where space allows—where he relaxes to look over his book until the rest of the class is ready to leave. There is an informality and pleasure about sprawling on the floor that the child does not experience when sitting at a table (Figure 1–10).

When the last name and room number are printed, the last card stamped, the last bookmark passed out, the librarian tells the children that they may take the books home and keep them until the next library visit. She shows them the correct place to return books.

Where the library checks out books to kindergartners, the procedure followed would be the same as described in Steps 4 and 5 above, the only change being that kindergartners would need to print only the first name and room number.

For rainy days, the children are asked to bring plastic bags, or the librarian may have on hand the large used envelopes she saves from the school mail.

Figure 1–10.

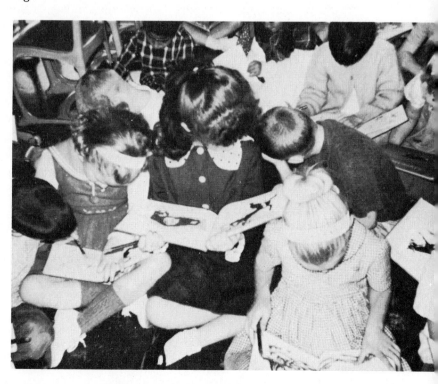

Grade 2

Step 1—At the beginning of the second grade, Willie and Debra again have a review lesson on the procedure for checking out books using the large sample tagboard card which several children fill in to remind the class of the proper form. They discuss the importance of returning books to the designated place and not anywhere else. Any book brought in and left on a library table or put on a shelf without the card is a "lost" book. The card in the file indicates the child still has the book. The book has to be returned to the book drop or given directly to the librarian. She explains what is done before the book is ready to circulate again: the book card is taken out of the file and returned to the pocket, thus clearing the child's record and making the book available for others.

ON THEIR WAY

When the second graders check out books, each child, with the librarian's help, stamps his own card and date slip. Since the librarian has so little time to guide an entire second grade class in book selection during the class period, she can do this in a time set aside for free browsing for second graders who come in in small groups instead of as a whole class. Reviewing books during story hour, displaying books on counters or tables, and posting book jackets also help the child in his selection.

Step 2—At the beginning of the year, the second graders are oriented to the Easy corner and reminded that here are the books of greatest interest to them. They are taught that the letter under the E on the spine of each book is significant both as an author letter and a guide to the alphabetical arrangement on the shelves (presented at length in Chapter 2, *The 26 Letters*) . To reinforce the concept, the librarian has each child give his full title and then state the letter that would occur on a book *he* might write. Following this, the librarian states the full name and author of each book she reviews. The children then state the letter that would appear under the E.

The Easy books need to have lettering that is consistent, e.g., an E above each author letter, to make the lesson on the location and arrangement of these books meaningful to the children.

Step 3—Willie and Debra have several practice lessons in reading the Easy shelves and in shelving Easy books. The librarian calls attention to the fact that the same letter is on the book card, the pocket, and the spine.

Before asking the children to read these shelves, the librarian needs to remember that since Easy picture books are of all sizes and thicknesses, children have great difficulty in handling and manipulating them on the shelves. The books constantly fall or slide. Children have trouble pulling out the books they want. To eliminate these irritations, the library need only add dividers, spaced at ten-to-fifteen-inch intervals.

Children checking out books or helping with desk routines, such as putting cards in order, will see the correlation of these letters when they appear in these three places. This becomes an essential part of their mastery of library skills.

Step 4—After becoming acquainted with the Easy center, second graders learn about and use other areas in the library. They spend a period among the fairy tales and listen to reviews of some of the titles. Other sections with which they become familiar at this time are space, dinosaurs, rocks, Indians, and poetry. And, as they become aware of these, they discuss the difference between fiction and non-fiction.

They further learn where pencils, pencil boxes, and colored paper bookmarks are kept, and where to put their signed book cards. When they finish second grade, they know where to go in the library to sharpen a pencil and where to go, alas, to spit out that gum!

TRANSITION

Because formal library instruction is scheduled for third grade through sixth, only a general overall view is presented here. Details occur step by step in the chapters that follow.

Grade 3

The third graders review essential points covered in second grade and have two sessions in reading the Easy shelves and shelving the Easy books.

In later lessons, they locate the set of *The Golden Book Encyclopedia,* become acquainted with and check out such magazines as

The Golden Magazine and *Highlights for Children,* and they begin to take an interest in and start using the vertical file.

Extensive instruction in alphabetizing authors, titles, and subjects lays the groundwork for the future use of the card catalog. Willie and Debra learn that this piece of furniture contains trays of cards which represent all the books in the library.

They begin to associate the Dewey classification number, the address of a book, in the upper left hand corner of the catalog card with the location of that number on the shelf. They have practice in the order of the Dewey numbers on the shelves. As third graders, they are concerned only with the part that is the whole number.

Their curiosity about the unabridged ("big") dictionary is satisfied when they compare it in size and content with the small classroom dictionary.

Third graders Willie and Debra are ready to assist at the checkout desk. Each third grader has a turn at stamping books for his class during several library visits throughout the year. Some are so capable at this that working in pairs they take over this responsibility while the librarian guides children in book selection. (See Figure 1–11.)

Figure 1–11.

STRETCHING THE VIEW

Grade 4

Willie and Debra in fourth grade learn the meaning of the word *blueprint* as related to a building. The transfer is made to the arrangement of materials in the library. One approach is to use a large tagboard blueprint which outlines the plan of the library. Labels in various colors are tacked on it to identify the areas they are familiar with and see on the blueprint:

Easy section	Pencil sharpener
Circulation desk	Book return
Fire exit	398's, 520's

and other centers of interest and need to the fourth grader.

Then various children go to the named areas, pointing them out to the rest of the class. This is the informal approach, later reinforced with lessons on the classification of books. These sections are further stressed in their relationship to those already located: e.g., what books are shelved across the room from the Easy books? Which next to the encyclopedias? Or, if a block of books such as fairy tales has been transferred out of the normal position, where are they in relation to another block of books? Children may be completely unaware of such relationships until their attention is called to them.

Each child may be asked to stand at a certain section and name its location. When he calls out "921's," the librarian adds, "Thank you, Mr. Biography," or for "977.3," "Thank you, Miss Illinois." Thus, early in the fourth grade, Willie and Debra have a picture of the areas of importance to them.

Early in the school year, all fourth graders, as well as fifth and sixth graders, receive a dittoed sheet on library regulations:

SOME THINGS TO KNOW ABOUT THE LIBRARY

1. Library hours for boys and girls are:

   . . . .

2. You may come to the library *once* during each recess time, remaining the full recess period if you wish.

3. You may take books home.

4. You may have . . . . . . leisure reading books out of the library at one time. Additional books may be checked out as needed for reports.

---

5. Books are checked out for . . . . . . weeks.
6. You are responsible for any books you sign out. Undue damage or loss of books is costly.
7. Write or print *legibly* your first and last names and homeroom for checkout:

| Sept. 21 | John Jones | 21 |

8. Return books before or on the date due.
9. Books may be renewed. Bring the book with you for renewal.
10. Reference tools, such as encyclopedias, may be checked out for overnight use:
    Check out after school
    Return these at 8:30 the following school day
11. Back issues of magazines go out for three days.
12. Pictures and pamphlets in the vertical file are ordinarily used in the library but may be borrowed for classroom use, or for several days.
13. When a scheduled class is in session in the library, reference people work independently. This is one time talking and whispering are taboo.
14. Hands are expected to be clean.
15. Books you reserve are held for you one day.
16. The librarian's office is off limits unless you are assigned to work there.

The librarian goes over these rules with each class. This is a good post-summer review for returning students and places the new ones at ease. The children are asked to keep this sheet in a library folder as a guide to the use of the library.

Grade 5

In the fifth grade Willie and Debra again use the blueprint they started with in the previous year (Figure 1–12). After they locate these areas in the library, they mask-tape the colored labels on the blueprint. Reinforcing their sense of security and independence in the library environment in this way, they can now "show the new kid the works."

Since much of this is a repeat for most of the class, it can be done in one period before the class plunges into a comprehensive grasp of the card catalog and other units, with considerable use of visual materials.

Figure 1–12.

Grade 6

Because of possible changes and the addition of new faces, the sixth graders like the fifth have a quick oral review of the library blueprint. Or, the librarian may hand out dittoed blueprints and each child may go about the library labeling his own copy. This is merely the beginning of a comprehensive coverage of the library: reference tools and skills, filing rules for the card catalog, etc., with detailed instruction and drill on the Dewey Decimal System review occurring early in the school year.

RECAPITULATION

A librarian may frequently inject new elements into the grade instruction, elements which change and cannot be placed in any particular category. Children are interested in all new things about them. (See Figure 1–13.) They may talk about the globe or an exhibit in the glass case or on the counter where dioramas or other student work and hobbies are displayed. Sometimes they discuss a bulletin board and the reason for a special display, the aquarium, or the posted book jackets or posters. Special holidays often produce divergent but instructive displays and discussions.

Figure 1–13.

As the children progress from the primary to the intermediate grades, the Easy section gives way in importance to other fiction, non-fiction, and reference. The card catalog looms larger and larger. The unabridged dictionary becomes a tool to use, not just a huge book with fascinating color plates. The contents of the vertical file are no longer a mystery, but are sources of information for reports. The simple *Golden Book Encyclopedia* is left behind for the *World Book* and for other reference works, such as the *Lincoln Library* and the *National Geographics*.

Suggested library skills and their sequence by grade level occur in the following chart, with these possible blocks of time:

    Kindergarten—Grade 1 .... 20 minutes
    Grade 2 .... 30 minutes
    Grade 3 .... 45 minutes
    Grades 4, 5, 6 .... 50 minutes
    Reference .... minimum 30 minutes

The 45- and 50-minute periods cover both instruction and checking out books.

SEQUENCE OF LIBRARY SKILLS

The grade levels suggested in this chart are for the *formal* presentation of each unit of library skills. The chart does not point out where reference to the unit is first made but does indicate subsequent levels for review.

	K	1st	2nd	3rd	4th	5th	6th
Good citizenship	X	X	X	X	X	X	X
Literature appreciation	X	X	X	X	X	X	X
Book care and handling	X	X	X	X	X	X	X
How to check out books	X	X	X	X			
Shelving Easy books			X	X			
Map work			X	X	X	X	X
Arrangement of fiction and non-fiction, including shelving				X	X	X	X
Alphabetizing to the fourth letter				X	X		
Alphabetizing authors, titles, subjects				X	X	X	X
Dewey Decimal System				X	X	X	X
Blueprint or floor plan of the library					X	X	X
Book indexes					X	X	X
Almanacs					X	X	X
Britannica Jr. Encyclopaedia					X		
Dictionary work					X	X	X
Card catalog usage				X	X	X	X
Card catalog filing rules				X	X	X	X
Reference skills other than bibliography							X
Atlases					X	X	X
Gazetteers						X	X
Parts of a book					X	X	X
National Geographic indexes						X	X
World Book Encyclopedia					X	X	X
Compton's Pictured Encyclopedia						X	X
Bibliography							X
Specialized reference tools, including *Lincoln Library*							X

From fourth grade on, with occasional directions, the children can manage the desk routine of checkouts. This is not always as simple as it sounds when many voices clamor, "May I work at the desk today?" "I didn't get a turn last time." "I've *never* had my turn." The election of a class captain who appoints stampers and monitors helps solve the problem.

Stamping and checking in books are routines children enjoy performing. Through these tasks they become acquainted with many book titles and begin to see the correlation between the call number on the pocket and the card, and that on the spine, whether the book be fiction or non-fiction. They become aware of the relationship between the classification number and the subject when they stamp books as well as when they check them in. Most of all, it gives them a sense of importance and responsibility.

The better organized the library is, the greater is the opportunity for the child to see the logical arrangement of library materials. Instruction and usage will help the child realize the value of these. All this is useful knowledge he will carry on to the high school library, the college library, and the public library.

Chapter 2—

The 26 Letters—

How to Teach

Alphabetizing

"Children do use the library without knowing the alphabet thoroughly," someone will argue. "They really can get along all right if they just know their A B C's." There is no denying this in the elementary sense. Second graders, with a few exceptions, can recite the alphabet and apply it in a primary situation. But to relate their understanding of the alphabet to a new setting requires much manipulation because the library and its use revolve around more than just reciting the A B C's. Use of the card catalog, reference books, indexes, and locating fiction books all involve the understanding and application of the alphabet, considerably beyond first-letter alphabetizing.

Grade 2

Step 1—If the physical arrangement of the library permits, the second graders may be seated before the Easy center, which is that part of the library most familiar to them, where they see the labels of A B C for each cubby or section of picture books (Figure 2–1). In preparation for reading the Easy shelves, the second graders first recite the alphabet while the librarian prints it on the chalkboard. Then she points out, e.g., the letter B on the B cubbies and reads several titles and last names of authors of books from this section. "What does the B stand for?" she asks. Several pairs of eyes and

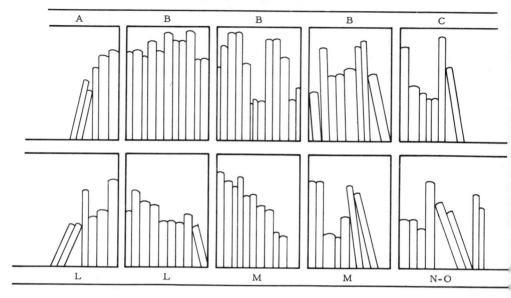

Figure 2–1.

ears will inevitably see and hear the relationship between the names read and the B on each spine.

"The author's name," reply Willie and Debra, echoing several other voices.

"Yes, exactly," confirms the librarian. Giving another example, she asks, "Which part of the author's name?"

"The last name."

The
Story
of
Ping
•
•
Flack
•
•
E
F

"Correct you are. Now, what do we call this part of the book where you see the author letter printed?"

"The back."

"Which part of the back? . . . Notice this part runs down the center of the back. What do you call the bones that run down the center of your back?"

"Backbone . . . spine," say several voices.

"Spine is correct, and that's what we call this part of the book. The author letters are on the spines."

The librarian continues, "Notice the books in the Easy center have two letters on the spine." By reading or holding up samples, as illustrated in Figure 2–2, for the second graders to see, the librarian asks, "Which one of these letters is always the same?"

After the answer, "E," she continues, opening the cover of the book to demonstrate, "That E you will see on the pocket and card in each book too. What does it stand for?" After this is cleared, the class reviews again the significance of the bottom letter.

Finally the librarian suggests, "Before we start reading the shelves to see whether all the books in a particular cubby belong there according to the author's last name, let's practice a little. Willie Rowan has just written a book on a trip to the moon. When we receive a copy of his book in the library, what letter will go on the spine?"

"R for Rowan."

"Good! Now each of you give your first and last names and the letter that would appear on the spine of a book you might write."

Figure 2–2.

Gag	The	Lenski
the	Country	the
ABC	Bunny	Little
Bunny	. . .	Auto
	Heyward	
E	E	E
G	H	L

Step 2—After a brief review of the previous lesson, the second graders turn back to the Easy shelves to watch a demonstration first on how to align the books right side up, spine out and even with the edge of the shelf. Then each child reads a cubby to see whether the authors' letters in it are all the same. If the collection is small, some children may double check the work of the first group. They learn to place over-sized books with the spines up so anyone pulling any one of these slightly out would see the letters near the tail of the spine.

In reading the cubbies, children pull out any books with a letter different from the one they're working with. They have been told that often various fiction and non–fiction books are placed on display in the Easy center for their enjoyment. When they spot these intruders on the Easy shelves, they remove them to the display counter or the tables. The librarian and the teacher check their work.

Step 3—After aligning the Easy books and making any necessary corrections in shelving, the second graders practice shelving Easy books, putting them in the proper cubbies according to the authors' letters. Their enthusiasm in such new situations of learning enables them to grasp quickly the concept involved so that soon they get along comfortably in the Easy corner of the library: essential groundwork for the coming year.

Grade 3

Throughout the year third graders come to the library for formal instruction, with frequent breaks for storytelling to allow the library disciplines to be absorbed. The children arrive with a classroom background in the use of the alphabet and previous library experiences. Most of them know how to alphabetize by the second letter, and some, at least, of their classmates can work with third- and fourth-place letters. Applying the alphabet in the library is a reinforcement of classroom work and *vice versa,* with the classroom work preparing the children for more detailed work in library skills. It is helpful to explain to a third grade class why such intensive groundwork in the alphabet is necessary. It will become evident to them once they begin to manipulate the books at the shelves and use the card catalog in the framework of the alphabet.

Step 1—The third graders start the twenty-six letters in the fall with a review, using simple, homemade flash cards. The class first locates the letter that comes *after* the one on the card being held up; it may then locate the letter that comes before. Each child has a turn, and a snappy, fast moving pace helps eliminate boredom with this routine work.

They then move to the Easy center to read the shelves there. Since they have already had experience with this routine in grade two, they work with confidence and pride.

Frequently they will come in during the noon browsing period or after school to inquire if they may shelve Easy books and read these shelves. They enjoy being helpers, and in so doing they pause often to browse. Their security in this skill also allows the librarian some extra time to turn to the more professional duties of reading guidance.

Step 2—After the review exercise in the Easy center, each child receives a pack of fifteen cards with authors' names. Now begins the real test of the child's knowledge of the alphabet, for some names given begin with the same initial letter. The third grader alphabetizes the cards from left to right. Only the last names are given as illustrated. The cards are, of course, shuffled before the child receives them to alphabetize.

| Burton | Politi | Coatsworth | Cleary | Slobodkin |

Step 3—The third graders alphabetize a list of authors including third- or fourth-place letters, such as the following:

Alphabetize these fiction authors—	
Gag, Wanda	. . . .
Buck, Pearl	. . . .
Burton, Virginia	. . . .
Bannerman, Helen	. . . .
Bannon, Laura	. . . .
Hays, Wilma P.	. . . .
Steiner, Charlotte	. . . .
Haywood, Carolyn	. . . .
Hayes, Florence	. . . .
Credle, Ellis	. . . .
Duvoisin, Roger	. . . .

After the children have completed their lists, they alphabetize the same authors on the flannelboard or chalkboard and check their written work.

Step 4—A sheet of sixteen samples duplicating the spines of books may be effectively used. The titles selected may reflect the reading interests of the particular grade.

With these sheets in front of them, the third graders first discuss and clarify the significance of the call number, correlating the author letter and the author. The next step is to differentiate between the publisher and the author on the spine. The children learn that the

CREDLE.. Down, Down the Mountain	Rudyard Kipling JUST SO STORIES	MRS. PIGGLE-WIGGLE McDonald	MARY POPPINS • • • TRAVERS	BAUM THE WIZARD OF OZ	B IS FOR BETSY • Haywood
Fic C	Fic K	Fic M	Fic T	Fic B	Fic H
Nelson	Garden City	Lippincott	Harcourt	Grosset	Harcourt

upper name is usually the author. This can as a rule be verified by checking against the author letter.[1]

As each names the author letter and the author thus:

>   Fic   B is for Baum,
>   B

the author is posted alphabetically on the board.

Step 5—Each child receives a pack of twelve of these same spines, cut individually. He arranges them on the table in proper alphabetical order by author. The librarian and the teacher move about to check the alphabetizing and give praise and guidance. At the end of the lesson each one shuffles and rubberbands his pack for other classes to use. (See Figure 2–3.)

Step 6—Several stacks of twelve books each are placed on the tables. The third graders working in pairs alphabetize these between bookends. The librarian and teacher again move about to guide the children. Once the stack of books is in correct order, the children involved attempt to shelve the books alphabetically with the collection

---

[1] Librarians whose schools meet American Library Association standards may wish to use the Cutter-Sanborn letter from now on.

Figure 2–3.

on the shelves. A colored strip juts out of each book thus shelved so the librarian may check it.

Step 7—The children are given individual cards with the name of the author and the title of a book which each is to locate on the shelves. With this previous preparation, third graders are no longer bewildered and confused when confronted with a sea of fiction. It is worth all the practice when Debra finds the actual book she is searching for and looks up with a grin of complete triumph on her face and announces jubilantly: "Look, I *found* it!"

Step 8—Before turning to the alphabetical arrangement of the card catalog, the librarian briefs the third graders once more on the last name first, whether it's looking on the shelf for a book of fiction or the name in the card catalog. By now most children will have grasped the concept that in alphabetizing, the author's last name appears first, followed by a comma:

Wilder, Laura Ingalls.

From a list of authors' names on the chalkboard each child states which part of the name appears first on the author card in the card catalog.

Step 9—Manipulating the twenty-six letters now involves alphabetizing titles. On the board are posted titles which the class arranges in alphabetical order. One of the children may list on the chalkboard enough of each title—usually just the first word—to show the alphabetical arrangement.

Inch by Inch	*Blueberries . . .*
Henry Huggins	*Charlotte's . . .*
Charlotte's Web	*Henry . . .*
Once a Mouse	*Inch . . .*
Mike Mulligan and His Steam Shovel	*Mike . . .*
Blueberries for Sal	*Mike's . . .*
Mike's House	*Once . . .*

Step 10—The children are introduced to the three exceptions: *A, An, The* are omitted when any one of these is the first word of a title. The children alphabetize the titles listed on the board, e.g.,

The Long-Nosed Princess
An Old-Fashioned Girl
A Filly for Joan
A Cap for Mul Chand
The Little Wooden Doll
An Adventure in Astronomy

Step 11—The children practice with packs of cards made up of authors and titles.

The Little Island
Burton, Virginia
Politi, Leo
The Little House

A Dog for Susie
Anderson, Clarence W.
The Real Mother Goose
Munari, Bruno
Geisel, Theodore Seuss
An Old-Fashioned Girl

Step 12—At their next library visit, third grade classes find on the chalkboard a list of twenty-six subjects all in capital letters,[2] one for each letter of the alphabet, all of them words familiar to the children.

BIRDS	ELEPHANTS
INDIANS	GOATS
PARKS	ZOO
CATS	JETS
QUEENS	VALENTINE
MAMMALS	OCEAN
X-RAYS	KITES
ALLIGATORS	YELLOWSTONE PARK
TOYS	UNITED STATES
HORSES	WEATHER
DOGS	NATURE
RACCOONS	SCHOOLS
LEAVES	FIRE

The librarian explains that each one of these words is the SUBJECT of a book in the library, and that each word will be found on the top line of a card or cards in the card catalog.

---

2 Not all libraries enter the subject on a subject card in capital letters. Librarians will need to adjust the wording to fit the method used.

Figure 2–4.

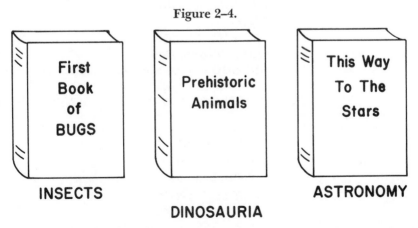

INSECTS   ASTRONOMY

DINOSAURIA

The librarian holds up several books with titles related to some of the SUBJECTS on the board. She reads each title and indicates the subject for it. She then holds up several more titles, this time asking the children to select the subjects. (See Figure 2–4.)

*Step 13—*The class then alphabetizes the list of subjects by the first letter of the word.

This list, in correct alphabetical order, is already on the chalkboard at the next class lesson. Beside it is a second list of subjects, titles, and authors which the class orally interfiles with the first list, by the second letter of the word:

AERONAUTICS	The Apple and the Arrow
Charlotte's Web	Gag, Wanda
JAPAN	WISCONSIN—FICTION
AUTOMOBILES	Andersen, H. C.

*Step 14—*The next lesson involves third- and fourth-letter alphabetizing using blocks of three or four words with the first and second letters the same, and occasionally the first three letters the same:

EAR	DOG	BAT
EASTER	DOLL	BALL
EARTH	DONKEY	BASEBALL

The children alphabetize each block of words as a block. The concept, "Nothing always comes before something," may be introduced here, using such examples as

EAR	SEA	FIRE
EARTH	SEASON	FIREMEN

*Step 15—*The children alphabetize a mixed list of SUBJECT words posted on the board. This entails alphabetizing by first, second, third, and fourth letter as the case requires.

*Step 16—*The final test involves alphabetizing subject, author, and title cards as they appear in the card catalog. The children work in pairs with stacks of 3 x 5 cards, twelve to a pack, which they lay out on the table in alphabetical order.

At long last, after many weeks of preparation, the third graders

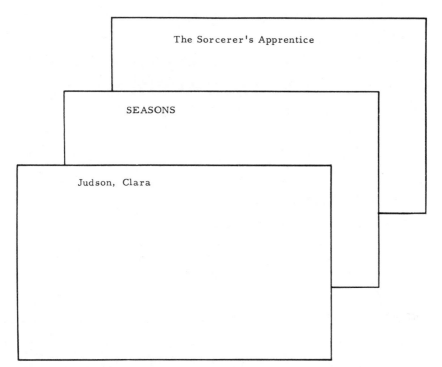

can meaningfully plunge their itchy fingers into the card catalog—another step toward self-reliance in the library.

Grade 4

Step 1—Fourth graders, after a summer's relaxation, need a refresher in alphabetizing. One way to tickle their fancy is to have, e.g., Willie Rowan stand, giving his full name as it appears on the name tag which he holds up. The next child to rise does likewise and stands to the right or left of Willie in alphabetical position according to the last name—and so on. When the whole class is lined up, each one, in alphabetical order, states his last name only and returns to his seat.

Step 2—In preparation for intensive work in the card catalog, fourth graders learn a few of the finer points of alphabetizing, such as the handling of abbreviations and numbers when one of these is the first word of a title. They learn to "Spell it out in your head, Willie!" Posted on the chalkboard may be a list of titles containing numbers and abbreviations to be alphabetized:

> *Mrs. Piggle-Wiggle*
> *Mr. Duck's Big Day*
> *Dr. Dan, the Bandage Man*
> *3 Little Pigs*
> *St. George and the Dragon*

Step 3—Chalkboard, flannelboard, and dittoed seat work are necessary; the titles starting with numbers and abbreviations are mixed in with subject and author cards.

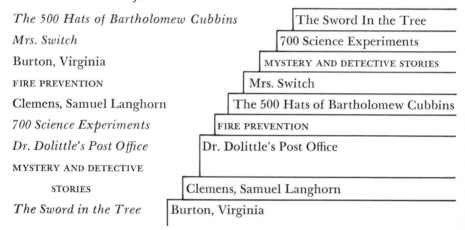

The 500 Hats of Bartholomew Cubbins	The Sword In the Tree
Mrs. Switch	700 Science Experiments
Burton, Virginia	MYSTERY AND DETECTIVE STORIES
FIRE PREVENTION	Mrs. Switch
Clemens, Samuel Langhorn	The 500 Hats of Bartholomew Cubbins
700 Science Experiments	FIRE PREVENTION
Dr. Dolittle's Post Office	Dr. Dolittle's Post Office
MYSTERY AND DETECTIVE STORIES	Clemens, Samuel Langhorn
The Sword in the Tree	Burton, Virginia

Grade 5

Step 1—Fifth graders may start out with one session on reading fiction shelves, and throughout the year those who wish may have the opportunity to alphabetize the daily fiction circulation.

Step 2—Alphabetizing rules are now reviewed as:

1. Alphabetize according to the top line of the card.
2. Omit *A, An,* and *The* when they are the first words of titles.
3. Spell out numbers and abbreviations.

The librarian checks for clean hands before she issues to each child a pack of twelve actual catalog cards to alphabetize. These may be cards for new books. Hence, this preliminary alphabetizing and filing will familiarize the fifth graders with new titles in the library.

Grade 6

Step 1—Sixth graders review rules for alphabetizing carefully before applying them.

RULES FOR FILING IN THE CARD CATALOG

1. Alphabetical arrangement by the *first* line.

2. Ignore *A, An, The* when one of these is the first word of a title.
   Example: The Call of the Wild is filed as if it were *Call of the Wild.*
   But in *A Apple Pie,* the *A* is counted, as it is *not* an article.

3. Spell out abbreviations and numbers.
   Example: Mc as *Mac*   Mr. as *Mister*   Dr. as *Doctor*
   Mrs. as *Mistress*   St. as *Saint*   500 as *Five Hundred*

4. Arrange all books by the same author alphabetically *by title,* regardless of variations in author's name.
   Example: Alcott, Louisa M.
      Little Men
     Alcott, Louisa
      Little Women
     Alcott, Louisa May
      Rose in Bloom

5. On the first line, when the *same* word appears as an author, a subject, a title: the *author* cards *come first.*
   Example: Homes, Gerald   (author)
     HOMES
     Homes of the American Presidents   (title)

6. *Ignore* all punctuation, such as hyphens (-), dashes (—), semicolons (;), colons (:), and commas (,) (except for the author card).
   Example: ANIMALS
     ANIMALS, ANCIENT
     ANIMALS—CARE
     ANIMALS, DOMESTIC
     ANIMALS—STORIES

7. Ignore all lines after the first line when the first line differs.
   a. Remember that nothing comes before something.
    Example: ANIMAL
      Animal Weapons
      ANIMALS
      ANIMALS—ALASKA
   b. File the shorter word before the longer, where they begin with the same letters.
    Example: With the Mounties   *Ann Rutledge*
      Within the Circle   *Anna and the King of Siam*

Each child receives a dittoed list of these rules for future reference.

Step 2—The class spends one period reading the card catalog for errors, as described in Chapter 8, the Card Catalog.

Step 3—Besides preliminary alphabetizing of catalog cards for new books, the children do preliminary filing *above the rod* in the card catalog (Figure 2–5) .

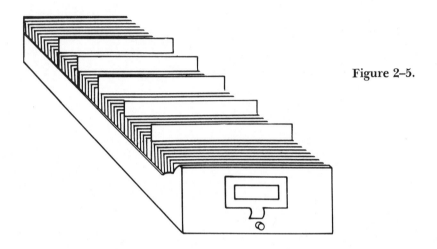

Figure 2–5.

The librarian of course checks the filing before dropping the cards into the trays and locking them in with the rod.

By now it is apparent that a broad use of many library materials rests on an understanding of the alphabet far beyond a simple ability to recite the A B C's. The card catalog, the dictionary, encyclopedias, fiction books, indexes, and many reference works are involved. With such groundwork, students going on to higher levels of study will find this discipline has become second-nature. Others may feel at ease in frequenting the public library, may confidently approach the librarian for help, and are more apt to have a sense of security in using these facilities.

Chapter 3—

Dr. Johnson's Legacy—

Learning to Use the

Dictionary

The dictionary is a reference tool that needs an early introduction. Many children avoid using a dictionary. Because it is difficult for them to locate the answers a dictionary provides, they find it easier to skip it entirely. Furthermore, a dictionary seems dull to a child. It is a thick book with words close together, sometimes in quite fine print; the abridged editions used in classrooms do not have very interesting or exciting pictures; often the definition of a word is couched in terms which to the child are as baffling as the word he is looking up.

In most elementary schools a beginning study of the dictionary in the library starts at the beginning of the fourth grade, though these children may have had some exposure to dictionary work in the late third grade. Competence in handling this reference tool depends on daily use, constant drill and practice, and consultation whenever a point arises in the classroom which the dictionary can answer. The length of time necessary for a complete dictionary unit is not usually available in the library skills curriculum; however, when a teacher requests the librarian to present an extensive dictionary unit,[1] the following basic information may be considered:

1. Spellings
2. Pronunciations
3. Derivations
4. Definitions
5. Antonyms and synonyms
6. Homonyms
7. Diacritical marks

Grade 4

As a change of pace from classroom instruction in the same subject, the librarian may introduce this unit as a changing, colorful collection of material with words that are interesting and fun to know about. Such an approach is only supplementary enrichment to classroom instruction and is in no way intended to replace it. It may, or may not, be followed by instruction in the basic skills mentioned above, according to the needs and wishes of the classroom teacher. Kipling's *How the Alphabet Was Made* is a stimulating beginning for this unit.

Step 1—"Hello, boys and girls," the librarian greets a fourth grade class one day in early winter. The children look faintly startled, not being used to quite such an offhand welcome. "You all know," continues the librarian, "exactly what I mean when I say 'hello' to you. I don't have to explain it. But if you had lived a hundred years ago, none of you would ever have heard that word. People greeted each other by saying, 'How do you do?' or 'Good morning.' And then in 1874 a man named Alexander Graham Bell invented something which to people living then was like a miracle. That invention was . . . ?"

"The telephone," a chorus answers.

"People became so excited at talking into this instrument to someone they couldn't even see that they didn't take time to say 'Good morning. How are you today?' They would shout into the telephone, 'Hollo! Hollo!' and this word finally turned into the 'hello' that we know today."

The librarian may then elaborate on the theme that language is by

---

[1] The following pamphlets, published by Scott, Foresman and Company, Chicago, are interesting and useful to a teacher or librarian giving instruction in a dictionary unit:

    What Goes Into a Dictionary (1965)
    Once Upon a Word (1966)
    W. Cabell Greet, *Pageant of Words* (1966)

no means dead, but because of new inventions and discoveries it is changing constantly. Even some slang words and expressions may, through long use, finally become respectable enough to be included in the dictionary, e.g.,

dough—money
rubberneck—to look all around
scram—get out quickly
G. I. Joe—an enlisted man in the United States armed services

In 1828 the last word in Noah Webster's dictionary was "zygomatic"[2] (having to do with the cheekbone). Since then, more than seventy new words follow this one. If the dictionary the class is using has a New Words section, the class may turn to it to see for themselves the kinds of words that are being added:

astronaut
television
refrigerator
windshield

On the other hand, there are words that go out of common usage. When the librarian asks the class how many have heard the word "victrola" the chances are not a hand will go up.

The librarian may then write on the chalkboard several words that she knows are too new to be in the dictionary the children are using and asks the class to look for them. When they realize these words are not in their dictionaries, the librarian tells them that the words came into use after their dictionary was printed. Children may offer words and then check to see whether they are included in the edition being used. Most children know of Mary Poppins either through the book or through the motion picture, and it will amuse them to know that Mary Poppins introduced the word *supercalifragilisticexpialidocious.*[3]

Step 2—The children find a large political map of Europe hanging on the wall when the lesson starts. The librarian first asks them which part of the world their ancestors came from. Everyone has something to contribute to this discussion. The librarian then selects three common names and, pointing to the proper country on the map, indicates what that name would be if its owner still lived there:

---

[2] From the pamphlet *What Goes Into a Dictionary?* Reprinted by permission of Scott, Foresman and Company.

[3] From the pamphlet *Once Upon a Word.* Reprinted by permission of Scott, Foresman and Company.

Country	Name		
England-United States	William[4]	John	Mary
France	Guillaume[4]	Jean	Marie
Spain	Guillermo[4]	Juan	Maria
Russia	Vilygelym	Ivan	Marya
Italy	Guglielmo[4]	Giovanni	Maria
Germany	Wilhelm[4]	Johann	Maria

She then points out that just as every boy and girl in the class has ancestors who came from other countries (unless someone is a pure-blooded American Indian!), so many words used every day are of foreign origin. It is unfortunate that beginning dictionaries do not usually have word derivations.

As the librarian indicates the origin of the following words, she hands a child a ticket with a flick of masking tape on the back. The child affixes the ticket to the country from which the words came:

Dutch	French	Spanish	German	Italian
coleslaw	prairie	tomato	frankfurter	spaghetti
cooky	gopher	chocolate	ouch	ravioli
waffle	chowder	canoe	kindergarten	pizza

Children are also interested in knowing that people's names sometimes become common everyday words:

> *sandwich:* The Earl of Sandwich was an English nobleman. He was an extremely hard worker and he so disliked being interrupted that he requested that food be brought to him while he worked—a slab of meat or cheese between two slices of bread.
>
> *pasteurize:* Louis Pasteur, a French scientist, invented a system of heating and cooling milk, which killed the harmful germs in it. This system is known as pasteurization.
>
> *watt:* James Watt was a Scottish scientist who, besides developing the first steam engine, discovered many things about power. Today electric power is measured in watts.
>
> *levis:* Levi Strauss of San Francisco, California, developed this particular kind of work pants.

The children may wish to add other words. Those who are interested might make a list to be looked up in a dictionary which does contain word derivations. Among those which may be used for this

---

[4] From the pamphlet *Once Upon a Word.* Reprinted by permission of Scott, Foresman and Company.

purpose are *Webster's Third New International Dictionary*[5] and *Britannica World Language Dictionary.*

    Step 3—The librarian tells the class that while many of our words are very new, many of them are very old. She may have on the board the development of a word, but omitting the final current English form. (See Figure 3–1.)

IXΘYΣ

Figure 3–1.

PISCIS

    She points out how one word grew from another and asks the class what the current word is. The children, of course, answer "fish" but acknowledge they would not have known if it had not been for the pictographs. The librarian questions the class as to the modern use of pictographs, using an arrow as an example. She may elicit X for a railroad crossing, a red cross for first aid, or various directional signs used on highways. To conclude her remarks she may draw a valentine on the chalkboard and ask the class to read it (Figure 3–2).

Figure 3–2.

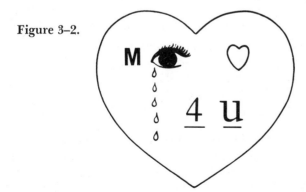

---

    [5] Titles cited are to illustrate specific points. These titles do not necessarily represent the most recent edition.

The librarian then explains that while the pictures mean something to the eye, this is not a means of communication with someone else. The symbol must be translated into a *meaningful sound,* which makes a word: a collection of letters which, when pronounced, conveys a meaning to someone else. It is possible to have symbols which can be pronounced but still do not mean anything to us. "Suppose," says the librarian, "Willie asks Debra if she wants some candy, and Debra answers 'trung.' Does Willie have any idea whether Debra wants any candy or not?" The children's answer is, of course, no. The librarian explains, " 'Trung' is a sound, but it is not meaningful to us."

We can see from this how important words are. If we had no words, it would be much more difficult to ask questions or give answers. It is of course possible to communicate by such signs as the deaf and dumb use, but this is not the concern here. Without words, it is unlikely that newspapers, books, and magazines would be as common as they are. Words are necessary tools for almost everything that is done in the world.[6] However, being able to use a word and knowing its meaning are what give it value. Don't use these words unless you know what you are talking about!

Chargoggagoggmanchauggagoggchaubunagungamaugg[7] (a lake in Massachusetts). It means "You fish on your side of the lake and I'll fish on mine."

Llanfairpwllgwyngyllgogerychwyrndrobwllllantysiliogogogoch[7] (a town in Wales)

Floccipaucinihilipilification[7] (estimating as worthless)

Step 4—Many different dictionaries are set up on a library table. Some of those displayed (listed alphabetically by title) may be the following:

1. P. D. Eastman, *The Cat in the Hat Beginner Book Dictionary* (New York: Random House, Inc., 1964).
2. Stuart A. Courtis, et al., *The Courtis-Watters Illustrated Golden Dictionary for Young Readers* (New York: Simon and Schuster, Inc., Publishers, n.d.).

---

[6] Material for this section was taken from Sam and Beryl Epstein, *The First Book of Words, Their Family Histories* (Boston: D. C. Heath and Company, 1954) and Leslie Waller, *A Book to Begin On, Our American Language* (New York: Holt, Rinehart and Winston, 1960).

[7] From the pamphlet *Once Upon a Word.* Reprinted by permission of Scott, Foresman and Company.

3. *Funk and Wagnall's Standard Dictionary of the English Language, International Edition Combined with Britannica World Language Dictionary.* 2 vols. (Chicago: Encyclopaedia Britannica, Inc., 1960).
4. Ellen Wales Walpole, *The Golden Dictionary* (New York: Simon and Schuster, Inc., Publishers, 1944).
5. Dilla W. MacBean, *Picture Book Dictionary with a Picture Story* (Chicago: Children's Press, Inc., 1952).
6. Wendell W. Wright, *The Rainbow Dictionary* (Cleveland: The World Publishing Company, 1947).
7. E. L. Thorndike and Clarence L. Barnhart, *Thorndike-Barnhart Beginning Dictionary* (Chicago: Scott, Foresman and Company, n.d.).
8. E. L. Thorndike and Clarence L. Barnhart, *Thorndike-Barnhart Junior Dictionary* (Chicago: Scott, Foresman and Company, n.d.).
9. G. & C. Merriam, *Webster's Elementary Dictionary for Boys and Girls* (Springfield, Massachusetts: Merriam Company, n.d.).
10. G. & C. Merriam, *Webster's New Practical School Dictionary* (Springfield, Massachusetts: Merriam Co., 1964).
11. G. & C. Merriam, *Webster's Seventh New Collegiate Dictionary* (Springfield, Massachusetts: Merriam Co., 1963).
12. Philip Babcock Gove, ed., *Webster's Third New International Dictionary of the English Language Unabridged* (Springfield, Massachusetts: G. & C. Merriam Company, Publishers, 1961).

These range from a picture dictionary to an unabridged. This is an opportune time to stress the words *abridged* and *unabridged.* The difference between these two words may be fixed in the minds of the children by such questions as "What is a bridge? . . . Its purpose? How would one reach the other side of a river without a bridge, without swimming, or without any other shortcut?" The children finally realize the need to go the long way round, even to the degree of encircling the river. Hence, an unabridged dictionary they realize encompasses all the words of the language. (See Figure 3–3.)

The librarian talks briefly about the different abridged dictionaries for the different grade levels, pointing out that the unabridged dictionary is the final source. She makes a comparison of the amount of material found for a main entry, e.g., *parrot,* in several dictionaries:

Webster's New Practical School Dictionary, 1964 ...... 8 lines
Webster's New World Dictionary—Elementary Edition, 1961 .... 11 lines

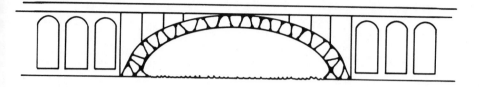

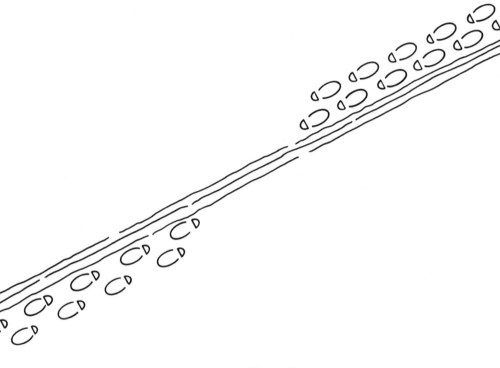

Figure 3–3.

Webster's Third New International Dictionary
of the English Language, Unabridged, 1961 ...... 30 lines

She may then ask the class how many have ever played the game of having someone describe an object or a person, and everyone else guess what it is. When almost every hand is raised, the librarian suggests the class try to describe a dictionary so that it is obvious to a listener that the description is of a dictionary. As the words tumble out, they are jotted on the chalkboard, among them "alphabetical," "list of words," and "guide words." The librarian cautions that if she heard only these, the answer might be an index. The children soon see their own words need to be more explicit. When all the words anyone can think of are posted, the class uses them to formulate a definition that includes the basic information a dictionary offers.

Step 5—The librarian gives the class "shortcuts" in looking up words. Each child opens his dictionary to the middle. Most children will find they have opened to the M's. They split the first half to discover D and the last half to discover S as follows:

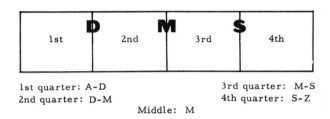

1st quarter: A-D   3rd quarter: M-S
2nd quarter: D-M   4th quarter: S-Z
              Middle: M

When this division is established, the librarian calls out various guide words. The child raises one finger for a word in the first quarter; two fingers for the second quarter; three for the third; or four for the fourth. For an M word, each one wriggles two fingers on one hand.

By this time the children are aware that there is something unusual about these words. Each word they have been looking up is at the top of the page. The librarian asks:

1. Where are the words located that you've checked so far?
2. What are they called?
3. Why are they called guide words?
4. Where are they defined on the page?
5. How may they help you locate words more quickly?

After discussing and locating guide words, the children continue looking up each word as it is written on the board. To challenge them the librarian checks the length of time it takes to locate a word, calling off fifteen seconds, thirty, forty-five, up to two minutes. This also encourages the children to think first in terms of what quarter the word will be in. Guide words are included in the lesson to train the children to look for these first.

The librarian may expand further on other phases of the dictionary, depending on time. A good little book to use with this material, and one which delights the children, is *Oodles of Noodles*[8] by Lucia and James L. Hymes, Jr. (Young Scott Books, 1964) which plays with words. Some of the nonsense rhymes can be used as illustrations of various points of dictionary usage. For example, to illustrate

   a. Spelling and pronunciation:

> *No! No!*
> *No, I know,*
> *Is spelled N—O.*
> *No, no:*
> *N—O, N—O*
> *So, so:*
> *S—O, S—O.*
> *Toe, toe:*
> *T—O? T—O?*
> *No! No! Add an E.*
>
> *Toe, toe:*
> *T—O—E.*
> *Foe, foe!*
> *F—O—E.*
> *Low, low:*
> *L—O—E?*
> *Noe? Noe? W.*
>
> *Low, low,*
> *Tow, tow,*
> *Row, row,*
> *Now I know.*
> *Low,*
> *Tow,*
> *Row,*
> *COW?*
> *Whoa, now!*
> *NO! NO!*

   b. Homonyms:

> *Nonsense*
>
> *You have no sense? You have no cents?*
> *Too bad! But I won't tell.*
> *But did you say you have no scents?*
> *Cheer up! You do not smell!*

---

8 Three poems from *Oodles of Noodles* by Lucia and James L. Hymes, Jr. Copyright 1964; copyright owners Lucia and James L. Hymes, Jr. Permission to quote granted by the Publisher, William R. Scott, Inc.

c. Slang:

> *Watch Your Language*
>
> *"Dis and dat"*
> *And "dese and dose"*
> *Are slang*
> *And very rough talk.*
>
> *Dish and Dot*
> *And Deeds and Doze*
> *Are fine*
> *And good enough talk.*

Further excursions into dictionary skills may be pursued if the teacher so desires. The World Book transparencies, *Learning "Look-it-up" Skills with a Dictionary,* will clarify a number of points. Skills discussed in the library (such as definitions, use of guide words, antonyms, synonyms, homonyms, etc.) may be completed through exercise sheets in the classroom under the supervision of the teacher. The "How to Use Your Dictionary" section of the 1952 edition of the *Thorndike-Barnhart Beginning Dictionary* has excellent exercises which may be adapted for the purpose. These are suitable for use also with other dictionaries such as *Webster's Elementary Dictionary for Boys and Girls.* Examples of the types of exercises which may be given students are as follows:

Example 1:[9] Here are the names of four animals:

    1. Otter   3. Squirrel
    2. Llama   4. Beaver

Read what the dictionary says about each animal. Answer these questions:

1. Where does a squirrel live? ....
2. In what country does a llama live? ....
3. Which animal can build dams? ....
4. What does an otter eat? ....
5. Does a llama have a hump? ....

Example 2: Answer the questions below by writing "Yes" or "No" after each one. You will need to look up the underlined word.

1. Can a *centaur* be found in a zoo? ....
2. Is a *grackle* a kind of noise? ....
3. Is a *limerick* a kind of soft drink? ....

---

[9] All examples are from the *Thorndike-Barnhart Beginning Dictionary.* Copyright © 1964 by Scott, Foresman and Company. Reprinted by permission.

4. Is a *puffin* a small pillow? ....

5. Can you drive a *hurricane?* ....

Example 3: Here are two guide words on one page of the dictionary:

glass	–284–	glue

Do the following words come
  a. before the first guide word?
  b. after the second guide word?
  c. between the two guide words?

globe .... glad .... gleam ....
give .... gold .... good ....

Example 4: Write a synonym for each of the following words:

1. succor ....   5. horrid ....
2. murky ....   6. pallid ....
3. morose ....   7. malady ....
4. valor ....   8. vivacious ....

Example 5: Write a sentence using each of the following homonyms:

1. flower ....
   flour ....
2. see ....
   sea ....
3. pair ....
   pear ....
4. heal ....
   heel ....

The filmstrip, *Stories Behind Words,* is a satisfactory conclusion for this unit.[10]

Grade 5

Step 1—For their first lesson on dictionaries, the fifth graders are given a brief history of this reference tool to stimulate interest in the subject. Samuel Johnson, the eighteenth century English lexicographer, who produced the first real English dictionary, was possessed of idiosyncrasies fascinating to all ages: his inability to work on his book without his ill-fitting wig perched on his head;[11] his

---

[10] *Stories Behind Words.* Curriculum Films, 1951. 3rd ed., 18th printing. 29 fr. color (Language Arts Series).

[11] From the pamphlet *What Goes Into a Dictionary?* Reprinted by permission of Scott, Foresman and Company.

often humorous and frequently biased definitions, occasionally quoted today:

> OATS:a grain which in England is generally given to horses, but in Scotland supports the people.[12]

From an account of Samuel Johnson the discussion goes on to the first American dictionary-maker, Noah Webster, who lived in the last half of the eighteenth and early nineteenth centuries. Reference to his role in developing the dictionary leads naturally into the examination of *Webster's . . . New International Dictionary of the English Language, Unabridged.*[13]

Step 2—If the group is sufficiently advanced, word derivations may be discussed here. The children's attention should be drawn to the placement of the current meaning of a word and the fact that this placement may differ in different dictionaries. *Webster's . . . New International Dictionary of the English Language, . . .* gives the oldest meaning first; *Funk and Wagnall's New Standard Dictionary . . .* gives it last.

The class examines in the unabridged dictionary the introductory material as well as the signs and symbols section, abbreviations, forms of address, the gazetteer and biographical sections in the back of the book. Since the entire class obviously cannot do this together, samples or illustrations may be presented on the flannelboard, the overhead projector, or the chalkboard.

Grade 6

Sixth graders study specialized dictionaries. The discussion on these occurs in Chapter 9.

Many opportunities arise naturally in the classroom for reinforcing dictionary work. These may be formal through instruction or incidental as the need arises. Students need to be encouraged to consult the dictionary throughout each school year.

---

12 E. L. McAdams, Jr. and George Milne, *Johnson's Dictionary, A Modern Selection* (New York: Pantheon Books, 1963).
13 The particular edition may vary from library to library.

Chapter 4—

Encircling the Arts and Sciences—

Getting the Most from Encyclopedias

The primary grades begin their practical use of the encyclopedia with the single volume, pictured *Golden Encyclopedia.* They may check it out of the library along with other picture books. They may also have several copies of it available for reference in the classroom.

Grade 3

By the third grade, Willie and Debra's curiosity is great enough that use of the *Golden Book Encyclopedia* by Bertha Morris Parker may be formally introduced in the classroom. These illustrated volumes give the children experience with the guide words and the index for simple reference to volume and pages. This set is a good preliminary introduction to the formal instruction that follows in the library.

Grade 4

Such preliminary experience is pertinent because the new fourth graders are sometimes abruptly plunged into encyclopedia reference work. To avoid their laments of "Teacher, I can't find this in the encyclopedia" . . . "This isn't in the encyclopedia" . . . "I can't work this index," the librarian needs to be ready to present instruction on the encyclopedia early in the year.

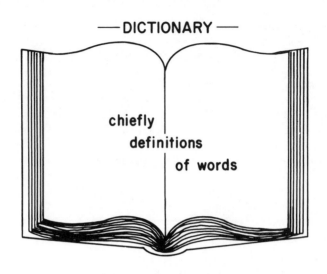

— DICTIONARY —

chiefly
definitions
of words

— ENCYCLOPEDIA —

A	B	C	D	E	F	GH	I J K	L	M	NO	P	QR	S	T	UV	WX YZ

Detailed Information

Figure 4–1.

Step 1—Several skills associated with dictionary instruction lead naturally into encyclopedia usage. Drill on alphabetical order, use of guide words, and use of the phrase "main entry" are equally applicable to the dictionary and the encyclopedia.

The fourth graders first make a comparison between the encyclopedia and the dictionary. Both have the following similarities:

1. The entries are in alphabetical order.
2. Both have guide words.
3. The entries are in bold-face type.

After a discussion of these similarities, the children begin to realize there is a major difference (Figure 4–1). They can readily realize the function of each tool by comparing the information each gives on such main entries as *flower* or *bird* (Figure 4–2).

Figure 4–2.

Thorndike-Barnhart Beginning Dictionary, Scott, Foresman, 1964, p. 267.
Flower (flou'er)[1] 1. Blossom. The flower is the part of a plant or tree
which produces the seed. Flowers are often beautifully colored or
shaped. 2. a plant grown for its blossoms. 3. produce flowers; bloom;
cover with flowers. 4. the finest part of a thing. The flower of the land
would be killed by a war. 5. the time when a thing is at its best. 6. be
at its best.

Britannica Jr., 1965, Vol. 6: 129–133.
Over four pages of description and discussion of the following:

> From Flower to Fruit
> Pollination
> Importance of Flowers in Plant Classification
> Uses of Flowers
> Care of Cut Flowers

In addition, four full pages of illustrations in color.

Step 2—In studying the index of *Britannica Jr.,* the children
view an index page on the opaque or overhead projector. Dittoed
copies giving a sample section from the index may also be used with
permission from the publisher.

Step 3—The filmstrip on *Compton's Pictured Encyclopedia*
is very effective for clarifying the same points:

1. An *entry* is a listed subject.
2. The *order* of the main entries is alphabetical.
3. The main entries are in bold-face type, while sub-topics are in
   lighter type.
4. *Sub-topics* are subjects indented under the main entry as they are
   part of the main subject.
5. The sub-topics under each main entry are in alphabetical order.
6. The letters and numbers in each reference refer to *volume and
   page;* e.g.,
   > 8–52a . . . . . . volume 8, page 52, column a.
   > C–64 . . . . . . volume C, page 64.
7. The comma in a reference means *and,* while the hyphen means
   everything in between; e.g.,
   > D–26, 30, 51 . . . . . . 3 pages in volume D.
   > H–26–51 . . . . 26 pages in volume H, starting with page
   > 26 and ending with 51.

---

[1] From the *Thorndike-Barnhart Beginning Dictionary.* Copyright 1964 by Scott,
Foresman and Company. Reprinted by permission.

8. A *reference* is made up of two parts: *volume and page.*
9. The index often refers the user to anywhere from one to ten or more references on the same subject.

This last question receives considerable emphasis in order for the child to realize that

    a. Information may be in a volume completely different from the one he would expect, as in *Compton's* 1966:S . . .

> Saturn, a planet P–354, 350.[2]

    b. Several volumes contain information on the same subject; e.g., *Britannica Jr.* 1965: vol.1 . . .

> ODYSSEY (ŏd'ĭ sē) Greek epic
> . . . . . . 11–207a; author 7–181b;
> Circe 4–300b; epic 5–340b;
> folklore 6–140Da . . . . Latin literature
> 9–74a; poetry 12–237a; Troy 14–178a; . . . .

    c. There is a difference between the *see* and the *see also* references; *Britannica Jr.* 1965: vol. 1 . . .

> AGRICULTURE (ag'ri kul'tur) farm industry, raising of crops and animals 2–89G . . . see also FARMING AND FARM LIFE and under names of specific crops, states and countries.

> JACKS see JACKSTONES.

> N.A.C.A. see NATIONAL ADVISORY COMMITTEE FOR AERONAUTICS.

> OIL (PETROLEUM) see PETROLEUM.

Step 4—Since the *Britannica Jr.* has only one volume as the index, the class is limited in practice. A class lesson then will of necessity send the children to the individual volumes. Cards, each with a different question, are passed out.

> *Britannica Jr.* 1965   Vol. . . . .
>   Page   . . . .
> 1. What are the four stages in the life history of an insect?

> *Britannica Jr.* 1965   Vol. . . . .
>   Page   . . . .
> 2. Name four types of Indian dwellings.

---

[2] Reprinted with permission of the copyright owner, F. E. Compton Co., division of Encyclopaedia Britannica, Inc., Chicago, Illinois.

Since the cards are used again and again in various classes, Willie and Debra copy their questions and look for the answers. They write the answers to the questions, adding the volume, page, and copyright.[3] Then they receive other questions.

As the fourth graders check the *Britannica Jr.* for answers to these questions, several will say, "But I can't find this subject in the encyclopedia." In order to stress the value of the index, the librarian will include questions whose answers are to be found only in the index itself, such as these fact entries from the *Britannica Jr.,* 1965, vol. 1. . . .

> GREENWICH (grĕn'ĭch or grĭn'ĭch)
> VILLAGE Bohemian quarter, S. and
> W. of Washington Square, N.Y.
> City; favored by poets, writers and
> painters.

> GREENWOOD LAKE largest lake in
> mountain region of northern New
> Jersey; bisected about equally by
> New York state line; 10 mi. in
> length.

Hence, she will reply, "Check the index. That will tell you the answer." The children begin to realize that looking up a subject without the help of an index is time consuming and may lead to nothing.

Grade 5

Step 1—After a review of the *Britannica Jr.,* fifth graders Willie and Debra turn to other encyclopedias, naming the different types found in the library, such as *Compton's Pictured Encyclopedia* with an index in each volume and the *World Book* with its reading and study guide. It is important to have several sets in the library. These are placed on the tables so that the children see and compare them and verify the information which is in table form on the chalkboard:

---

[3] Later they will become aware this is the bibliographical form.

Britannica Jr.	*Compton's*	*World Book*
1. Volume 1 is the index for the whole set.	1. Each volume has an index.	1. No index, but a reading and study guide.
2. Alphabetical.	2. Alphabetical	2. Alphabetical.
3. Reference is to volume number.	3. Reference is to volume letter.	3. —

Step 2—As in grade four, the filmstrip frames or transparencies on *Compton's* Fact Index may also be effectively used to clarify the index references.

Step 3—To understand the index, the class uses Compton's KYE set,[4] which contains fifteen duplicate copies of an index column with complete explanation and practice questions. The class does written work on using the index, at first recording volumes and index pages on which the subjects are listed. (See Figures 4–3, 4–4, and 4–5.) They give several references each. No answers to questions

Figure 4–3.

---

[4] Copyright 1964 by F. E. Compton Co., Division of Encyclopaedia Britannica, Inc.

USING THE FACT-INDEX

There are three major uses of the Compton FACT-INDEX.

1. The FACT-INDEX is used to obtain brief information.

2. The FACT-INDEX is used to locate a single item of information.

3. The FACT-INDEX is used to locate *all* the information on a major topic.

Spotswood, or Spottswood, Alexander (1676–1740), American colonial governor, of Scottish descent, born Tangier, Africa; lieutenant governor of Virginia 1710–22; deputy postmaster general of colonies 1730–39; developed Virginia iron industry; aided education: P-342a

Sportsman's Sketches, A', by Ivan Turgenev T-296
spot, goody, or lafayette, a fish S-396
spot removal, from fabrics D-200d–f

Games G-8-14, *pictures* G-9-14. *See also in Index* Athletics; Play; Sports
babyhood to school days P-386, 389-90, *pictures* P-389-90
Bible mentions N-381b
billiards B-156, *picture* B-156
books about G-14, H-439
bowling B-281-2, *diagrams* B-282, *pictures* B-281
bowls B-282
cards, playing C-135-6
charades C-205
checkers C-227, *pictures* C-227
chess C-248-50, *diagrams* C-249, *picture* C-248
competition in leisure-time activities discouraged L-185
croquet C-614, *diagram* C-614
dominoes D-164-164a, *diagram* D-164a, *picture* D-164
etiquette, good sportsmanship E-306
horseshoes Q-18
instructions for active games G-10-12
marbles M-105, *picture* M-105
Middle Ages M-299
Olympic Games: ancient and modern O-451-4, *pictures* O-451-3
play P-385-90, *pictures* P-385-90
playgrounds and playfields P-127-8, *pictures* P-126-7
quoits Q-18
roque C-614
rules for quiet games G-12-14
table tennis, or Ping-pong T-1, *diagrams* T-1, *picture* T-1

The "gather-up" for the subject GAMES refers you to 10 of the 15 volumes of Compton's for information about games. The main article is in Volume GH. The subentries refer you to *9 other volumes* for additional information.

Figure 4-4.

Figure 4-5.

Canada, a nation of North America; 3,851,809 sq. mi.; pop. 18,238,247; cap. Ottawa C-70-100, *Fact Summary* C-87-96b, *maps* C-98-9, 72-3, 90, 93, N-308, F-417, *pictures* C-70-1, 74, 76-87, 96-96a, *Reference-Outline* C-96c-d, *table* C-76
agriculture C-80-1, A-111 *charts* C-92, *map* C-93, *pictures* C-71, 74; government aid C-81; maple sugar and syrup M-93; wheat. *See in Index* Wheat, *subhead* producing regions Canada
animal, national C-87, *picture* C-87
animals C-76, 77, 79: protection B-197, 203, C-77
area C-89: Europe compared, *chart* E-523; other countries compared, *charts* C-87, U-433
armed forces: uniforms and insignia U-334-5, *pictures* U-334-5; veterans' benefits V-610
armorial bearings F-207, *color picture* F-201
arts C-85
banks B-59d-60: Bank of Canada B-59d-60, *picture* B-59d
bibliography C-96d
boundary unfortified G-208, C-83
cable connections C-5, 7-8
capitals, history of C-96b
Capitol C-87, O-507, *pictures* O-507, C-70, 87, 90
cities C-96b, *map index* C-97, 100. *See also in Index* names of cities
citizenship C-357-8, *pictures* C-357-8
climate C-75-6, 88, P-145: animal and plant life varies with, *map* N-311; climatic regions, *map* C-88; temperature and precipitation. *graphs* C-88
coast lighting L-272
coastline C-89, *map* C-88
coat of arms C-87, *picture* C-87

St. Lawrence Seaway S-19, 20-1, *diagrams* S-19-20, *map* S-19, *picture* S-19, *color picture* U-367
steamers, *picture* C-71
tunnels. *See in Index* Tunnel, *table*
United States and C-83-4
vegetation C-76-7, *pictures* P-363e-f: varies with climate, *map* N-311
voting rights C-357-8
waterpower, *chart* C-94: resources

Kinds of entries

MAIN ENTRIES are printed in heavy black type. They are arranged in alphabetical order.

SUBENTRIES are listed under many main entries. The subentries are also in alphabetical order. They are indented and are printed in type that is thinner than the type used for main entries.

The special learning aids—maps, charts, graphs, diagrams, tables, Fact Summaries, and Reference-Outlines— are printed in *italics* for quick finding. Examples of these are underlined in the index section shown at the left.

What these entries do

Main Entries in the FACT-INDEX list the topics on which there is information in the encyclopedia. They direct you immediately to the information you are seeking, by listing the volumes and pages where the information may be found.

Subentries divide major topics into their parts or subtopics. They give volumes and pages for each subtopic. They enable you to locate definite bits of information at once.

Main entries with subentries make it possible for you to find *all* the information on each major topic. These entries are often called "gather-ups" because they gather together in one place all the volume and page references you need for finding all the facts about the major topic. For example, see the index section on Canada at the left.

are asked for at this point because the complete emphasis is on the value of turning to the index first. The following is an example from *Compton's* 1965:

A reference listed in the index consists of two parts:				
....and...				
COMPTON'S ENCYCLOPEDIA 19– (indicate set you are using)				

Subject	Where is the subject listed in the index?		List 3 references given on the index page for the subject:		
	volume	page			
ex:BIRDS	B	446	B–168–208	G–262	P–145
1.					
etc.					

Step 4—Each child receives an individual card with a different question. Again, as with the *Britannica Jr.,* each child copies his question and looks for the answer. With the teacher and the librarian working closely together, the questions in the drill can be correlated with the current unit of study in the classroom. For example:

(Name of encyclopedia & date)   **Volume** ....
                                        Page ....

OKEFENOKEE: What and where is it?

(Name of encyclopedia & date)   **Volume** ....
                                        Page ....

What contribution did Lewis and Clark make to American history?

Indicating on each card the edition of the encyclopedia to be used and having a variety of questions prevent any two children from using the same volume. When the pupil correctly completes the brief answer, giving the volume and page number on which he found it, the librarian initials it in red when it is correct and gives him another question. Each one works at his own pace.

Step 5—In studying the *World Book* the child compares the amount of information given here on one subject with that given in each of the other encyclopedias. Each one selects one of the subjects posted on the chalkboard.

Subject: FLOWER	No. of pp.	No. of pp. with pictures	Differences, if any
Britannica Jr. '65	10	7	4 full-page color
Compton's '57	20	19	12 full-page color and more analysis is given.
World Book '64	34	28	Over 14 in full color. Great detail on analysis and a section on pollination. Outline and bibliography. Pictures are related to festivals and customs.

Step 6—Since the *World Book* does not have an index, the approach to instruction is to direct the child to look under the specific topic; e.g., he would look for the topic SNAKES in the S volume. Transparencies are a good means of introducing the children to the *World Book,* with emphasis placed on cross references at the end of each article. After a question-and-answer period, individual questions are given to each child for direct use of the set.

Step 7—The librarian introduces a slightly different type of reference in *Our Wonderful World,* an encyclopedia anthology. Each of five main themes is made up of writings already published in that field, chosen for their interest and readability. The subjects are not arranged in alphabetical order but an excellent index is in the last volume, of which additional copies are available through the publisher.

As new specialized encyclopedias appear on the market, they will need to be evaluated. Reviews of these will occur in the professional literature, such as *The Booklist and Subscription Books Bulletin* issued by the American Library Association.

Step 8—Yearbooks are an essential addition to encyclopedias. They give new, detailed information on the highlights of the year and supplement the material already in the encyclopedia set. E.g., the *World Book Year Book* gives colorfully illustrated details of the most important events of the year. The index in each yearbook edition refers to various edition years, with the page numbers, such as:

Space travel 65–505, 64–488, 63–488 . . . .

Example from *World Book Year Book* 65–505–:[5]

---

[5] From *The World Book Year Book.* © 1965, Field Enterprises Educational Corporation.

> A PILOT, a physician, and a space scientist—Soviet citizens all—circled the earth 16 times on Oct. 12 and 13, 1964, to become the world's first multiman space crew.
>
> The three men, Colonel Vladimir M. Komarov, Lieutenant Boris B. Yegorov, and scientist Konstantin P. Feoktistov, made the journey in the spacecraft Voskhod (Sunrise). It lifted off from Baikonur in the Mayun-Kum Desert, Kazakhstan. One day and 17 minutes later, it landed 350 miles to the north, with the three still aboard. Their 72 man-hours in space brought the Soviet total to 455, which is nine times the number of hours chalked up by U.S. astronauts.
>
> (This goes on with illustrations for $7\frac{1}{2}$ pages.)

The index to the *Compton's* yearbook also refers to various edition years. But the page references following the entries and occurring in the order of importance are for the particular issue being used. The index is a five-year cumulative index. For example, from the 1963 edition:[6]

> Gemini, 223–4, 41

> Kennedy, John F (itzgerald) , 53, *pictures* 53, 227 [60–62]

The bracketed numbers indicate information in the editions for those years.

Step 9—Following the introduction on yearbooks, there will be individually written questions on each volume on hand. Since the number of yearbooks in a given library is apt to be limited, questions on these and on some other reference tool may be combined to constitute one period of drill.

Grade 6

Step 1—Sixth graders become acquainted with the *Britannica Book of the Year*, which is on an adult reading level and has considerable detail on the highlights of the preceding year only. The children look at copies of this reference tool or at a transparency on

---

[6] Reprinted with permission of the copyright owner, F. E. Compton Co., division of Encyclopaedia Britannica, Inc., Chicago, Illinois.

the overhead projector. The librarian queries the children on the following points:

1. The publication year is marked on the spine:
2. Subjects and numbers are given in bold-face and light-face type.
3. Letters a, b, c, d refer to sections of the page:
4. Subjects listed with no reference given appear in alphabetical order in the body of the book.

1961	
Events for 1960	

a	c
b	d

The children read samplings from the index and explain them (Figure 4-6).

Step 2—The class spends one period on individual questions, such as

> 1. According to the 1959 edition, how many miles is **WHITE ALICE**, a communications network in Alaska?

> 2. In 1962 how many times was the *Thor-Agena B* flown?

Step 3—The sixth graders now return to the *World Book Encyclopedia*. The librarian reviews for them, with the aid of the overhead projector, the *Reading and Study Guide*. This is a classification of the subject matter into numerous areas, such as biology, biography, medicine, sociology, etc. The children receive much individual help as the need arises in their regular reference assignments.

Step 4—The sixth graders turn now to the *Lincoln Library of Essential Information* which is also an encyclopedia. It comes in either one or two volumes with an excellent index. It is divided into twelve thumb-tabbed subjects:

Mathematics	Geography and travel
Government and politics	Science
Biography	Economics and useful arts
English language	Fine arts
Literature	Education
History	Miscellany

To be noted are the similarities to the ten classes of the Dewey

INDEX

The black type entries are article headings in this and previous issues of the *Book of the Year*. These black type article entries do not show page numbers because they are to be found in their alphabetical position in the body of the book, but they show the dates of the issues of the *Book of the Year* in which the articles appear. For example "Paris Big Four Conference of 1960–61" indicates that the article "Paris Big Four Conference of 1960" is to be found in the *1961 Book of the Year*.

The light type headings which are indented under black type article headings and cross references refer to material elsewhere in the text (of this issue only) related to the subject under which they are listed. The light type headings which are not indented refer to information in the text not given a special article. These refer to this issue only. Those which refer to the article **Obituaries** are followed by the date of issue in which the obituary appears. References to illustrations are preceded by the abbreviation "il."

All headings, whether consisting of a single word or more, are treated for the purpose of alphabetization as single complete headings. Names beginning with "Mc" and "Mac" are alphabetized as "Mac"; "St." is treated as "Saint." All references below show the exact quarter of the page by means of the letters *a*, *b*, *c*, and *d*, signifying respectively the upper and lower halves of the first column and the upper and lower halves of the second column.

Figure 4–6.

Decimal Classification. One will find information here that may be nowhere else in the library.

Further review of the *Lincoln Library* occurs in Chapter 9 where many specialized references are discussed to help the children in the intermediate grades with their extensive reference work.

Summary

Starting with *Britannica Jr.* in grade four, the children begin to apply their knowledge of how to use the encyclopedia. The more advanced fourth graders are capable of transferring this knowledge to *Compton's* index, while fifth graders are prepared to study the *Lincoln Library* or the *Book of Popular Science*. In mid-year they begin to feel quite at home with encyclopedias, and with help are willing to attempt the yearbooks, especially since many of these are colorfully illustrated. Finally, as sixth graders, the children include further reference tools to which they have briefly been exposed in the latter part of the fifth grade, such as almanacs, atlases, and yearbooks.

Chapter 5—

Reference Skills—

And How to Develop

Them

Note-taking, skimming, outlining, and bibliography are skills certainly needed for knowledgeable use of encyclopedias and other references. How much exposure a child has in the classroom will determine the structure of a library unit in such skills. Children who have had extensive classroom work will need only a reminder to jot down notes in their own words and to record the sources of their information. But those who are taught these skills chiefly in the library will need more than just a mention of the techniques involved and the generally accepted forms for doing so. This is most effectively done with small groups.

Though the child receives most of the formal instruction in reference skills in the sixth grade, he nevertheless needs to have simple directions on these as soon as he comes to the library for reference work, no matter how young he may be. It is easier to start correctly from the beginning, despite the time and effort involved, than to have to break later the bad habit of meaningless copying of words.

Grade 4

Step 1—At the teacher's request, the librarian may re-emphasize what note-taking means. Before the fourth graders select the encyclopedias or other materials to be used, the librarian may say, "Read the material first; then close the book and record the gist of what you have read; or better, do this paragraph by paragraph. Once you've read it, don't look at it, but write in your own words what it means to you. You may need to read the paragraph three or four times—grown-ups do that too—before you're ready to take notes on it. Follow this same procedure of note-taking for each paragraph or page you read. Then look over your notes, see how they fit together, and write your report. Remember to write down your source!"

A difficult assignment for fourth graders, but the potential capabilities of these children are often underestimated. *Plagiarism, the passing off as one's own another's ideas, words, writings, etc.,* is a case in point. Through discussion, the children indicate they *are* capable of comprehending it and of avoiding it by using direct quoting of excerpts.

During the reference work that follows, both the librarian and the teacher move about the room to give guidance to the children. The more practice Willie and Debra have, the better prepared they will be for the future.

After extensive practice in both library and classroom, each child reviews his written notes in preparation for an oral report to be given to the class without his using the written notes as a crutch. Willie will be reading for understanding and will more likely make sense to his listeners. At the same time, he is developing self-confidence and self-reliance. The value of taking notes in one's own words now has meaning.

Step 2—When fourth-grader Debra first appears to do reference work in the library, she is also given instructions on how to make a simple bibliography. She learns to write the source at the top of the page or card containing her notes: author and title (from the title page) and page numbers; e.g.,

Britannica Jr. 1965. vol. 13–3b   **Mary Jones**
Mason: *Animal Trails.* p. 11
RACCOONS
....
....
....

Reminders for such simple practice need to be given in the fifth and sixth grades.

Grade 5

Step 1—The librarian, in this unit, may explain the significance of note-taking, before reading aloud short, selected paragraphs from encyclopedias or books of fiction, biography, etc. After each paragraph is read, various children state the main idea in a *single* sentence and the class usually realizes which statement fits best.

Example 1 from *World Book,* 1967. vol. Q-R: 165:[1]

Much crop land that has become either too dry or too flooded for farming purposes can be *reclaimed* (restored to usefulness). Irrigation and drainage are two of the most common ways of reclaiming wasted lands. Removal of stumps from cutover forest lands and restoration of eroded land are also classed as reclamation.

Gist: Wasted lands can become useful again through irrigation, drainage, and clearing.

Example 2 from *World Book,* 1967. vol. Q-R: 300:[2]

Moth larvae called *stem borers* sometimes live in the stems of rice plants. Other insects suck the plant juices or chew the leaves. Birds eat ripening grain or newly sown seeds. Bird enemies of rice include the bobolink (sometimes called the ricebird) and the Java sparrow or paddybird. Fungi, tiny roundworms, viruses, and bacteria infect the plants and cause disease. A fungus disease called *blast* causes the panicles to break. Weeds, such as *barnyard grass (jungle rice), sedges,* and *red rice,* are common in rice fields.

Gist: Birds, insects, and bacteria are enemies of the rice plant.

Such exercises call for both brevity and conciseness. Of course, a library instruction period of twenty or thirty minutes a week is far too limiting for any extensive drill, but two or three effective lessons will reinforce similar practice that follows in the classroom.

Step 2—Brief instruction in footnoting[3] occurs in grade five. In the same period, the children learn to expand a bibliographical reference. To the author, title, and pages given in the bibliography,[4] they add the name of the publisher and the date. This process, which

---

[1] From *The World Book Encyclopedia.* © 1967 Field Enterprises Educational Corporation.

[2] From *The World Book Encyclopedia.* © 1967 Field Enterprises Educational Corporation.

[3] A footnote is a note at the foot of a page indicating the source of a quotation or of a piece of factual information.

[4] See page 53.

strengthens the concepts learned in grade four, helps establish the correct habits of taking notes and making bibliographies.

Grade 6

It is apparent from the previous discussion that formal instruction in reference skills is not undertaken in grades four or five. Incidental information for outlining, note-taking, and making a bibliography is mentioned only in connection with reference assignments.

Sixth graders, however, may be exposed to some detailed instruction in these skills.

Step 1—Although note-taking seems to be the most frequent method used in reference work, the children find that some material lends itself well to outlining. The librarian may present the outline approach through an informal talk on some particular subject in a form organized for outlining. In her introductory remarks she states the theme and indicates she expects to cover certain major points. (See Figure 5–1.) The children gain a sense of security by hearing how many points their outline will involve. The talk obviously needs to be highly organized so each child will be aware of each major point as it is introduced.

Figure 5–1. Outlining.

John Newbery

John Newbery was born in England on July 19, 1713. His father was a farmer but John had no taste for this life and was apprenticed to a printer in the nearby town. When the printer died, John took over his business.

In 1744 John Newbery moved to London and opened his own shop, called the *Bible and Sun*. He became a well-known bookseller and along with his books sold patent medicines, the most famous of which was "Dr. James's Fever Powder." In one of the books which John Newbery wrote and published, *Goody Two Shoes*, the heroine's father died because he could not get hold of any of Dr. James's Fever Powder.

John Newbery is famous as the first person in England to write and publish books for children which were to be read just for fun, instead of moral tracts children had been condemned to read because there were no other books for them.

John Newbery died in 1767.

John Newbery's name is best known today for the Newbery Award, given each year by the American Library Association for the most outstanding children's book published during the year. This award was made possible by an American publisher, Mr. Frederic G. Melcher, who became enthusiastic about books for boys and girls when he was a bookseller in Boston. The first Newbery Award was given in 1922 to Hendrik Van Loon for his book, *The Story of Mankind*.

Outline on John Newbery

I. Early life
   A. Born in England, 1713
   B. Father a farmer
   C. Apprenticed to a printer
II. Professional life
   A. Bought business when printer died
   B. 1744 moved to London
   C. Ran book shop and sold patent medicine
   D. Wrote and published many books
      note: Goody Two Shoes his most famous
III. Received fame because he was
   The first person in England to write and publish books for children to read for fun
IV. Died in 1767
V. Newbery Award
   A. Given annually by American Library Association to best work of literature for children
   B. Award donated by Frederic G. Melcher, American bookseller and publisher
   C. First award made in 1922 to Hendrik Van Loon for *The Story of Mankind.*

Some appropriate subjects to correlate with outlining, and also with note-taking, are

   a. History of the Newbery and/or Caldecott books:
     Lee Kingman, ed., *Caldecott Medal Books: 1956–1965* (Boston: Horn Book, Inc., 1965).
     Bertha M. Miller and Elinor W. Field, eds., *Newbery Medal Books: 1922–1955* (Boston: Horn Book, Inc., 1955).
     Bertha M. Miller and Elinor W. Field, eds., *Caldecott Medal Books: 1938–1957* (Boston: Horn Book, Inc., 1957).
     Irene Smith, *A History of the Newbery and Caldecott Medals* (New York: The Viking Press, 1957).
   b. How a book is made:
     Agnes Allen, *The Story of the Book* (London: Faber and Faber, 1952).

David Coxe Cooke, *How Books Are Made* (New York: Dodd, Mead & Company, Inc., 1963).

Hellmut Lehmann-Haupt, *The Life of the Book* (New York: Abelard-Schuman, Ltd., 1957).

Marshall McClintock, *Here Is a Book* (New York: The Vanguard Press, 1939).

c. History of books and printing:

Julie Forsyth Batchelor, *Communication: From Cave Writing to Television* (New York: Harcourt, Brace & World, Inc., 1953).

Rhys Carpenter, et al, *Everyday Life in Ancient Times* (Washington, D.C.: The National Geographic Society, 1961).

David Diringer, *Writing* (New York: F. A. Praeger, 1952).

Sam Epstein and Beryl Epstein, *The First Book of Printing* (New York: Franklin Watts, Inc., 1955).

Franklin Folsom, *The Language Book* (New York: Grosset & Dunlap, Inc., 1963).

Joanna Foster, *Pages, Pictures, and Print* (New York: Harcourt, Brace & World, Inc., 1958).

Keith Gordon Irwin, *The Romance of Writing* (New York: The Viking Press, Inc., 1956).

Daniel C. Knowlton, *Our Beginnings in the Past* (New York: American Book Company, 1933).

Enid L. Meadowcroft, *The Gift of the River* (New York: Thomas Y. Crowell Company, 1937).

Olive Beaupré Miller, *Picturesque Tale of Progress* (Chicago: Book House for Children, 1949), Vols. I, III, IV, V, VI, VII, VIII.

Oscar Ogg, *The 26 Letters* (New York: Thomas Y. Crowell Company, 1961).

Edward Osmond, *From Drumbeat to Tickertape* (New York: Criterion Books, Inc., 1960).

d. History of Libraries:

Julie Forsyth Batchelor, *Communications: From Cave Writing to Television* (New York: Harcourt, Brace & World, Inc., 1953).

Rhys Carpenter, et al, *Everyday Life in Ancient Times* (Washington, D.C.: The National Geographic Society, 1961).

Lincoln Library of Essential Information (Buffalo, New York: The Frontier Press Co., 1955).

Enid L. Meadowcroft, *The Gift of the River* (New York: Thomas Y. Crowell Company, 1937).

Olive Beaupré Miller, *Picturesque Tale of Progress* (Chicago: Book House for Children, 1949), Vols. II, III, IV, V, VI.

Frances Rogers, *Painted Rock to Printed Page* (Philadelphia: J. B. Lippincott Company, 1950).

In addition to these books, many of which are often part of the elementary school library collection, information on these subjects can be found in the standard encyclopedias.

After the librarian's talk, the class may first discuss the major points of the outline. Then the children jot down notes for each major point or they do reference work, supplying details to the outline. Thus, they may formally expand the outline which may culminate in a written or oral report. The natural conclusion of the activity is making a bibliography.

Step 2—"If a biography is the life of a person, what then is a bibliography?" asks the librarian.

"The death of a person?" ventures Debra, straight from the gifted workshop. Debra, along with all sixth graders, has probably heard the terms *biography* and *bibliography*, together with their meanings, on an average of once a week from the fourth grade on. Indeed, the term *biography* creeps into innumerable third grade conversations. Yet these terms, frequently as they are used, give constant trouble. Some children will still go into the seventh grade and tell the librarian that a bibliography is the life of a person or they need a biography at the the end of a report. Writing the origin of *biography* on the chalkboard may help clarify the difference. The strange Greek characters may fix the term correctly in mind:

βίός = life (as in <u>bio</u>logy) + ΥΡάφΟS = write

βίΟΥΡαφΟS = the writing of the life (of a person)

It is best to give the derivation of only the one word *biography* to avoid confusing the children with too much Greek!

Step 3—Each sixth grader receives a dittoed sheet containing bibliographical forms for books, encyclopedias, and magazines. Standard forms are introduced, uniform with those used in higher grades. Some variation, of course, occurs in the punctuation of bibliographical forms. The librarian points this out to the class and emphasizes that it does not greatly matter which form is used, as long as the author of the report is consistent.

It is helpful to have the forms for books, encyclopedias, and magazines on the board simultaneously. The flannelboard is as effective a tool here as it was in the card catalog unit. Various children post the different parts of the bibliographical form for books on the flannelboard. Others become critics, explaining why they agree or disagree. The same activity occurs with the forms for the encyclopedia and the periodical. The class compares the bibliographical forms to see the differences in arrangement:

Trade book
  author
  title
  publisher
  copyright date
  pages referred to

> Hegner, Robert. *Parade of the Animal Kingdom.* Macmillan, 1958. Pp. 190–92.

Encyclopedias
  title
  most recent copy-
    right date
  volume
  pages referred to

> *Compton's* 1965. Volume S: 223, 227. *Book of Popular Science,* 1965. Vol. 8: 220a.

National Geographics or
  other periodicals
  title
  date
  article
  volume
  pages referred to

> *National Geographic,* March, 1954. "Night Life in the Gulf Stream." Vol. 105: 391–418.

    Step 4—The lesson continues with the librarian placing several bibliographical forms incorrectly on the flannelboard. Each child writes the proper order for these on paper. Then the class makes the corrections on the flannelboard. Each one checks his own answers.

    Step 5—The children already know that the title page gives the author, title, publisher, and sometimes the date. If the date is not on the title page, it may occur on the verso. They go further to learn that

    a. Each article in the encyclopedia has a name.
    b. An author's name often appears at the end of an article.
    c. Not only the first volume but every volume in the encyclopedia set has its own title page.

They learn through inquiry to record the most recent copyright date. Magazine information is reviewed and a short written exercise, including a trade book, an encyclopedia, and a magazine, concludes the unit.

Each one is given a copy of the following:

WHEN YOU COME TO THE LIBRARY TO DO
REFERENCE WORK

1. Bring with you: Pencil
                    Eraser
                    Paper
   Any other material you think you may need: for example, a ruler.

2. Be sure you know what your subject is and the spelling of it.

3. First check the encyclopedia for your subject. Use more than one encyclopedia. The encyclopedias are located ....
   The World Book
   Compton's Pictured Encyclopedia
   Britannica Junior
   Our Wonderful World
   The Book of Popular Science

4. Next check the card catalog for SUBJECT cards on your subject. Find the call number (upper left corner of card). Go to the shelf to see if the book is there.

   If you don't find a SUBJECT card with your subject listed, think what larger group of things your subject belongs to:

   Example: A skunk is an animal. If you don't find a subject card for SKUNK, look for a subject card ANIMALS. Go to the shelf with the call number for ANIMALS. Look in the *index* of a book on animals for "skunk."

5. Check the pamphlet section of the vertical file for additional material.
   Remember:
   List the author, title, publisher, and page numbers of the book where you found your material.

   For an encyclopedia, write the name of the encyclopedia, year it was published (you will find this on the back of the title page), the name of the article you have read, the volume, and the page number the article was on.

   <u>Don't Copy</u>. Read the material, close the book, and write down in your own words what you have read!

   Before You Leave:
   Put all your material away where you found it.
   Push in your chair and leave a tidy table.

The significance of teaching reference skills cannot be over-emphasized when one realizes the difficulty confronting the majority of high school and college students in taking notes. By following the above lessons, the student avoids the undesirable pattern of copying information word for word, resulting in a plagiarized and often incoherent and disorganized report. The student will not need to struggle with manipulating excerpts from his readings when he is taught to read for understanding and to state the main ideas in his own words. He will learn to speak with force and meaning.

Chapter 6—

From Cover to Cover—

Discovering the Parts of

a Book

Information related to parts of a book filter through various library lessons in grades two and three. But it is not until fourth grade that formal instruction is given on the subject.

Grade 2

Step 1—As indicated in Chapter 2, second graders early in the fall start learning about the parts of a book. They start with the spine: "You have a spine, too, that runs down your back." They learn that books are always kept on the shelves with the spines facing out.

At this time they also learn that the spine has on it the author's name and the title of the book, as well as the inked E and author's initial which have earlier been pointed out to them.

Step 2—Several visits later the second graders become acquainted with the title page. On each table is a stack of books with titles appealing and suitable to grade two. When the librarian has identified for the class the title pages of several books, each child selects a book from his table and attempts to locate the title page. With help from the teacher and librarian, he reads aloud the author and title of his book.

Step 3—Presently the class discusses page numbers:

1. Pages are usually numbered at the bottom.

2. It is helpful to have pages numbered to find the place quickly in the book.

3. Some books have no page numbers.

The librarian may call out a page number, or the children may take turns doing so, and everyone locates the number as quickly as possible.

By the time Debra has finished second grade she is familiar with the library words:

> Author   Page number
> Title   Title page
> Spine

These words, then, are part of the library vocabulary of beginning third graders, who add to them:

> Illustrator   Call number
> Publisher   Fiction
> Binding   Non-fiction

Grade 3

Step 1—For locating books on the shelves and shelving books correctly, third graders need to be able to differentiate between author and publisher. Most third graders know the function of the author, and that of the publisher needs to be described in simple terms the first time the word appears. A fairly accurate rule for the children to follow is that, of the two names on the spine, the upper one is the author's and the bottom one the publisher's.

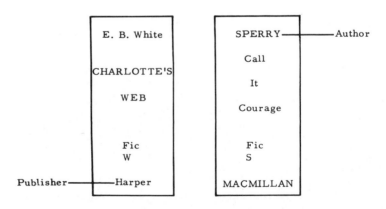

The class then has review in associating the author letter with the author's last name. Third graders originally learned this with Easy books. Now the children learn that the librarian is the one who prints the call number on the spine.

It may be mentioned that the top of the book is called the *head;* the bottom, the *tail;* and the trimmed leaves down the side of the book, the *fore edge* (Figure 6–1).

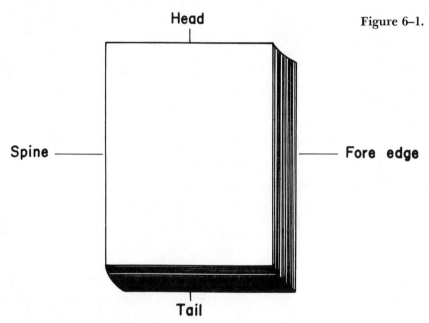

Figure 6–1.

Step 2—Willie and Debra and their classmates discuss the significance of the parts of the call number as information on a book spine: the symbol for fiction[1] and the classification number.

Large cards printed with a Dewey number associated with an appropriate picture may be displayed; sample books may be held up; and a trip to the shelves reinforces this concept. Here many books on stars may be seen, with 520 on the spine of each. Again the letter, representing the author's last name, is stressed.

Step 3—A display of books by fine illustrators is a natural opening for a discussion on the part an illustrator plays in a book's

---

[1] The symbol for 'Fiction' varies from one library to another.

Figure 6–2.

makeup (Figure 6–2). The children learn where this name is located in the book. For greater interest in this subject, the librarian may display original illustrations for children's books if such a collection is available.[2]

---

[2] Librarians working in California may request the Gladys English Memorial Exhibit on loan by writing to the State Library, Sacramento, California. This exhibit is in four sections. There is a charge for insurance and shipping costs.

Grade 4

Step 1—An exhibit on communication, with papyrus, clay tablets, wax tablets, and paper made from pressed wood pulp by library assistants arouses tremendous curiosity for children preparing for a unit on the parts of a book. (See Figures 6–3, 6–4, and 6–5.)

Figure 6–3.

Figure 6–4.

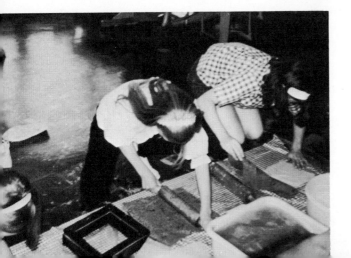

Figure 6–5.

In addition, there are samples of the papyrus plant, information on the Rosetta Stone, reprints from the Gutenberg Bible, and a copy of the tiniest book in the world containing the Lord's prayer in seven languages. Accompanying this display may be a collection of colorful foreign picture books, hornbooks and battledores, such as Figure 6–6 illustrates. In fact, an exhibit of any items of this nature will enrich this discussion. What more colorful introduction could Willie and Debra want for a lesson on the parts of a book?

Step 2—With a discussion of the objects on exhibit, including oral descriptions, from cave wall paintings to the modern volume, the librarian introduces an inquiry into the parts of a book: the main text itself, and the material preceding and following the main text. The discussion and explanation of these parts may cover two or three library visits. For this unit of work, Willie and his classmates bring their history texts to the library. These are well adapted to this study, for such books usually contain the parts that

HORNBOOK-
Printed paper glued
on a board and
covered with a thin
sheet of horn to
preserve it.

Figure 6-6.

BATTLEDORE -
used chiefly for
the game of
battledore or
shuttlecock.

are discussed. The librarian ascertains that each child turns to and actually looks at each item:

> PARTS OF A BOOK PRECEDING THE MAIN TEXT

1.   The *half-title* is a page which has on it only the title of the book.
2.   The *title page* contains the name of the author, the title of the book, the illustrator, and the series (if any) , the name of the publisher, the place of publication, often the year of publication, and frequently a picture. The title page, not the spine, is always the place to look for the author's full name and the complete title of the book.
3.   The *copyright date* may be on the title page but is often found on the *verso,* the technical term applied to the back of the title page.

Pointing to the word on the board, the librarian asks, "What does *copyright* mean? Turn it around . . . yes, *right copy* . . . *right to copy*. Do I have the right to copy and sell any book in this library? Why not? What would happen to me? If I should be found out, I might be taken to court and jailed.

"So, what does a copyright do for the author? . . . It protects him and gives him the right to the profits of his own creation.

"Does the author obtain this protection from the police? . . . from the government? . . . which government?" Through such a process of inquiry, the children finally deduce that the United States government grants the copyright. The librarian tells them the cost is four dollars to obtain a copyright for twenty-eight years and that this may be renewed for another twenty-eight years.

It needs to be pointed out here that the date of publication and the copyright date may not be the same, as it takes some time to go through the routine of registering a copyright. Often there are several copyright dates, the most recent one being the most important.

4. The *table of contents* lists the chapters of the book in order and gives the page on which each chapter starts.
5. The *introduction** by the author, or some other authority, gives a brief description of the book and why it was written. *Acknowledgments* to people who helped with the book are often included.
6. The *dedication*. If time is taken to discuss dedications, the children find it interesting to hear several dedications read. C. S. Lewis' book, *The Lion, the Witch, and the Wardrobe,* has a beautiful dedication.
7. A list of other books by the author.

PARTS OF A BOOK FOLLOWING THE MAIN TEXT

---

8. The *bibliography** is a list of references, related to the subject, which the author has consulted before writing his book.
9. The *index* is a list of subjects, alphabetically arranged, giving references which indicate the pages containing information on each subject.
10. The *appendix** contains facts and figures which are helpful in understanding the book, but not actually necessary to the book's use.

Items indicated by are not introduced until the fifth grade.

11. A *glossary* defines a list of technical or uncommon words used in the book. It is a little dictionary for that particular book.

12. A *key to abbreviations** is an explanation of any abbreviations used. It may be in the front or the back of the book.

Step 3—The librarian now introduces the *signature*. The easiest way to illustrate the signature is first to pass around a discarded book, with the cover gone. The children learn that each signature is made from a sheet of paper folded several times. They see the folds of the back section of the leaves. In most instances they can also see the sewing thread and flakes of glue which fastened the book into the casing.

Children usually assume a book is printed with the pages running consecutively and are surprised at how different and complicated the process really is. The pages of a book are printed in multiples of four, i.e., four pages on one side and four on the other; or eight on one side and eight on the other, etc. They watch a demonstration of the making of a signature.

The librarian folds a large sheet of newsprint in the middle and then in half, making a quarter. She numbers the squares within the folds as follows:

1	8
4	5

7	2
6	3

The sheet is held up so the class clearly sees how the numbers run. Then the librarian folds the sheet, cuts across the top, and presto! Like magic, the pages, as they are opened, run in consecutive order. Naturally, every child in the class will want to try this for himself. What better time than now? Go to it! (See Figures 6–7 and 6–8.)

Steps 4 and 5—A creative culmination for the entire unit is to have each child make a small booklet, starting with two flat sheets of newsprint, folding each into a quarto, stapling the two signatures together, and scissoring the top edge so the pages fall free. Or, instead of stapling these together in the library, the children may upon re-

Figure 6–7.

Figure 6–8.

turning to class sew the signatures together with a heavy duty needle and thread.

The children may refer to stories they are reading, or they may use their own names as authors and create their own titles to be printed on the front cover. Each one fills in the various parts of the "book:"

1. Half-title page
2. Title page, using the teacher's last name for the publisher, the city where the school is located as the place of publication, and the current year as the date of publication
3. Copyright on the verso
4. Dedication
5. Table of contents
6. Introduction
7. Index, and any other parts desired.

For the main text, each child may want to write his own story or give a summary of the book he is reading. If time allows, illustrations may be added. The library will want to display these booklets. Many of them will be highly imaginative, really creative pieces of work.

Grade 5

Step 1—The exhibit given above for the fourth grade furnishes ample background for a presentation on the history of a book from the development of printing in China to its discovery in Germany, and from the various writing media of cave walls to wood pulp. With an enthusiastic instructor, it could spill over into the classroom as an enrichment unit, covering a wide range of subjects:

Travels of paper from China to Italy
Printers' marks
Development of movable type
Books of Hours
Printing in America
Lives and contributions of such well-known printers as

Gutenberg	Caxton
Jensen	Morris
Aldus	Franklin

Encyclopedias are an adequate source for information on these subjects.

Step 2—In discussing the history of libraries, the librarian

may particularly describe what they were like in the early days when
the scarcity of books demanded that the patron wait in line to take
his turn at reading the book that was chained to a stand as illustrated
in Figure 6–9.

Then when printing was invented and "extensive" libraries developed, books could be borrowed. The meaning of "call number"
is explained in relation to the way books were shelved, protected,
and checked out.

At one time there were no public libraries, only private or university libraries. There were no open shelves of books in the university
libraries at which a patron could browse. He had to write his name

Figure 6–9.

and all necessary information on the book he wanted: title, author, and call number. This he got from a bulky one-volume catalog. He presented his *call slip* to the guardian or keeper of the books and was told to come back one, two, or three days later for the book. The book had to be tracked down as it might have been shelved or stored by color, size, shape, etc. The patron always had to wait several days after he turned in his *call slip*. From this process in which he *called* for his book comes the name *call number*.

Step 3—Willie and Debra as fifth graders review the parts of a book studied in the fourth grade, adding the starred items in the list given under grade four.

Step 4—The librarian introduces fifth graders to technical terms, according to the depth into which she wishes to go, and according to the capabilities of the class. E.g., the class may become familiar with the word *cased* and learn that today true binding, done by hand, usually in leather, is very expensive. Casing, on the other hand, is quite inexpensive. A casing is a sturdy piece of cardboard cut to the size of the book and covered with cloth or a plastic material which may be wiped clean with a damp cloth. The casing is glued to the leaves of the book, which have been sewn together, down the back edge. Children will be interested to examine an old handbound, leather-covered book, if one is available for showing.

The fifth graders learn that many printing terms used today are Latin terms that have come down to us from the time printing was invented in the fifteenth century because at that time Latin was the language of educated people.

In reviewing the signature, the fifth graders learn that when the sheets of a book are folded a certain number of times, Latin terms identify these as

> Folded once, making four pages: *folio*
> Folded twice, making eight pages: *quarto*
> Folded thrice, sixteen pages: *octavo*

Since the word "Latin" has little meaning for most elementary school children, the librarian may write a few Latin words on the chalkboard, and if she can still roll out Caesar's "Gallia est omnis divisa in partes tres," she is the sensation of the school.

As a conclusion to this unit, the class may visit the rare book collection of a local college or museum.

— TIPPING —

Figure 6–10.

Grade 6

Step 1—In the sixth grade demonstrations on book mending may occur:

Magic-mending torn pages
Squaring torn corners
Tipping pages (Figure 6–10)
Reinforcing outer backing with Mystik tape
Renewing entire torn back
Sewing loose signatures

Step 2—Sixth graders are taken through the steps involved in the physical production of a book, from the original idea of the book until it reaches the library shelves:

Research
Writing
Submission to publisher
Editing
Setting up in type
Problems of illustrations
Proofreading
Folding
Binding
Shipment (to book store or jobber)
Purchase by library

The film *The Story of a Book,* an account of the making of Holling's *Pagoo,* is a colorful and dramatic enactment of the early steps involved in this process. It makes a stimulating point of departure for Step 2.

This entire unit is one which particularly needs to be rich in visual aids. Flat pictures, filmstrips, and motion pictures are available. A trip to a local printing plant makes clear many processes it is almost impossible to describe in words to children who have never seen an old handpress, a modern printing press, a linotype machine, or a folding machine. A library exhibit may include a stick of hand-set type, a linotype slug, and galley proofs. Local newspapers and printing shops may be approached for the loan of these items.

Finally, an invitation to an author to speak to the group may complete this unit (Figure 6–11). Many authors are happy to lend samples of corrected manuscript, blown-up photographs from which

Figure 6–11.

By permission of the *Sunnyvale Standard Register Leader.*

book illustrations have been made, pages of galley proof, etc., and to discuss with the students the problems encountered in the production of their book.

Exposed to such an enriching unit, some children may for the first time really begin to appreciate books. Experiencing the processes of how a book is made may open whole new fields of thought to them.

Chapter 7—

Mr. Dewey Himself—

Learning the Dewey Decimal

System

Now it is Mr. Dewey's turn. For months the librarian has been telling the third graders, "Look in the star books, 520"—"It's in the 629's"—"Check the 590's on the top shelf"—"You'll find them on the shelf marked 560, dinosaurs." She is constantly giving out the Dewey numbers for various subjects as she points out the locations of the books. Indeed, for the primary grades, whenever a subject is mentioned the corresponding Dewey number may be given; or conversely, when a number is mentioned the subject may immediately be associated with it.

Grade 3

There are times during library periods when the third graders sit in front of the 600's and 700's or other Dewey classes while the librarian reviews the contents of some of these books. Simultaneously, she points out the numbers which correspond to the subjects:

614	first aid	780	music
636	pets	793	magic
640	cooking	796	sports

After such a session, these shelves begin to empty at checkout time.

Step 1—It is now time to introduce Mr. Dewey officially. Who was he? What did he contribute to the library? The children are intrigued to hear that there was a time when books were grouped according to color, size, shape, or accession number. They find it difficult to visualize books on all different subjects collected on the shelves simply by color. They learn that Melvil Dewey, at twenty-five years of age, after he was graduated from Amherst, was so irritated with the illogical arrangement of books that he developed a system by which all books can be classified by number into ten main groups. Since then, 1876, the system has been in use.

Step 2—On the board are posted the ten classes of the Dewey Decimal system. The children also receive a dittoed copy of these for their library folders. A discussion revolves around the first number of each class ending in two zeros and the last number of each ending in 99. The children note that the first digit of each number in both columns is in order from 0 to 9:

000–099
100–199
200–299
300–399
400–499
500–599
600–699
700–799
800–899
900–999

Step 3—A column of numbers, one from each Dewey class appears on the chalkboard. The children call these out orally in order as one child posts them on the board. They note that the order starts with the smallest number and ends with the largest. One may eliminate the last two digits of each to let the class see that the numbers are still in order by just the first digit.

636	0	3	0
973	1	7	7
220	2	2	0
398	3	9	8
741	4	2	3
423	5	2	3
811	6	3	6
523	7	4	1
030	8	1	1
177	9	7	3

Then the board is cleared.

Step 4—The librarian places two numbers from the same Dewey class on the board: 680, 612. The children respond on the order. They have had enough arithmetic in the classroom to know that one goes by the second digit when the first digits are the same. The class continues with examples such as 638, 610, 636. It's better to work across the board, left to right, rather than in a column, as many children tend to shelve from right to left. As the children call off each consecutive number, Willie writes it on the board according to the pattern on the shelves. Each number is separated by a dash. For example:

Place the following numbers in order:

660–940–598–510–292–556–979–808–508–030

Following this, with the cooperation of their teacher, the children have an arithmetic lesson related to the library instruction. They take copies of thirty or forty Dewey numbers back to the class, to be arranged in order. Beside each number on the copy is listed the subject:

Write the numbers in order:

220	Bible	549	rocks
574	nature	636	pets
520	stars	973	U.S. history
741	drawing	580	plants
599	mammals	352	policemen
796	baseball	383	stamps

Step 5—When the children return to the library the following week, they sit grouped on the floor in front of the non-fiction shelves. They have brought back the lessons, from which they enumerate the Dewey numbers orally. As each number and its subject are given, a child goes to the shelves to locate a representative book for that number. The children become aware as they answer the librarian's questions that the numbers become larger from left to right on each shelf and progressively so from section to section, that one constantly moves from the beginning at 000 to 999 at the end. Excitement is in the air as each child has a turn locating the particular number and subject named. E.g.,

500 — 502	589 — 590	599 — 621
502 — 539	590 — 591	623 — 629

The librarian points also to the labels on the shelves identifying certain large areas as stars, dinosaurs, plants, animals, pets, and drawing.

| 520 | ASTRONOMY |

In an alternative drill, the librarian may now hand a book to a child who becomes a "postman." The child reads the classification number on the book as 636. He and the librarian start searching in the 100 block, the librarian questioning as they go:

1. How does a postman know to which block of houses the catalog* goes?

   The correct answer makes the children realize that the classification numbers on the books already shelved take them to the right "block" or shelf.

2. The postman has many catalogs. How does he know which house to go to to leave each catalog?

   Here too, just as the number on the address leads the postman to the house with the same number, so the classification number leads the child to the correct section—and the child sees that many books standing together may have exactly the same "house number," or class.

Finally, the book is deposited in the right place to everyone's satisfaction.[1]

   Step 6—Class members now look for books by their addresses. Several catalog cards, enlarged to a 9 x 10 size are placed on each table. While one child points to the call number, another reads it aloud. This ensures all children in the class knowing what the number is. Willie's card reads as follows:

| 560 | *Beasts of the Tar Pits* |
| R | |

"Dinosaurs," the librarian remarks. And, if Willie happens to remember where he always locates the dinosaur books, he and his com-

---

[1] Our gratitude to Mrs. Gertrude Stacy, library supervisor in the Sunnyvale Elementary School District before her retirement in 1962, for permission to use this presentation, which she developed. Part of this material appears as an article by Gertrude Stacy in the April 1955 issue of *Wilson Library Bulletin*. It is used here with permission of the *Bulletin* © copyright 1955 by The H. W. Wilson Company.

* For explanation of word "catalog" see Chapter 8, p. 107.

panion will reach their destination quickly. Card in hand, the two of them travel together to the shelves to locate the "address." It is helpful to have a slower child work with a more capable one.

Debra knows from past library experience that the general arrangement of books is A to Z for fiction and 000–999 for non-fiction. Only the whole numbers and no decimals are taken into account in the third grade. She has learned in the blueprint of the library that the numbers on the shelves become larger from left to right and from one shelf to the next. Her previous experience enables Debra to participate knowledgeably in the activity.

Step 7—Following this, the third graders practice arranging non-fiction books in order, from left to right, between bookends on the tables. This parallels the drill with fiction books, except that now the books are arranged by the Dewey numbers. After every two children have read the shelf, one calls each number while the other records it in the order given. They check the recorded numbers for order. And the librarian can check these lists quickly. If time runs out, she can check these lists later and have them ready for the children the next week.

Step 8—Each child takes a card from a pack the librarian has available and, card in hand, goes to the shelves and attempts to locate the section which matches the call number on his card. When he locates the book, he turns its spine down on the shelf, leaving the card jutting from the fore edge. He waits for the librarian to check it.

In an alternative drill, book jackets for non-fiction may be marked with their proper call numbers and the children receive these to shelve. The jackets are readily visible and can be quickly checked for correct shelving. They are administratively and time-wise much easier to handle.

This is not an easy exercise for third graders. Confusion and frustration often ensue and much patience and help are needed from teacher and librarian before a child finally locates the spot he is seeking. More capable children, again, are frequently able to give assistance to slow ones.

Step 9—The class again sits in front of the non-fiction shelves, where the librarian has beforehand arranged several books out of order for the lesson. Two children at a time go to the shelves to look for a number that is at the wrong address. They read a shelf until they spot a book out of order. They reshelve the wandering book and read the numbers of three books, with the found book in the middle. The class decides whether the book is correctly shelved.

Step 10—The children take turns selecting a book from a stack on the table or from the book cart. The title and call number are read aloud to the class before a child attempts to shelve the book. If he goes in the wrong direction, or strays from the immediate address, his wiser classmates make all kinds of faces and with difficulty control their feelings. Sometimes they let go with, "Not there, silly!" or something much stronger. This is only human nature and learning self-discipline is part of the lesson. The librarian or various children may encourage the "postman" with, "Now you're getting warm, warmer. You're burning up!" or "You're freezing!"

Eventually the address of the book is located. The children note that the book is shelved next to a book with exactly the same number or follows a number that is smaller or precedes a number that is larger.

At no time in this process of learning numbers has the decimal concept entered. The children have worked only with the whole numbers.

The newness of the activity and the challenge of mastering the skill hold the attention of every child, especially when the location of the book is called the "address" of the book.

And so, the significance of the call number on a catalog card is established: its location *on the card, on the book,* and *on the shelf.*

Grade 4

Step 1—Fourth graders in the second semester receive a copy of the ten classes of the Dewey Decimal System with instructions to file these in their library folders:

DEWEY DECIMAL SYSTEM	
000–099 *General works* 　　　ex: encyclopedias,	500–599 *Pure Science* 　　　ex: astronomy, trees
100–199 *What men think* 　　　(philosophy)	600–699 *Applied science* 　　　ex: medicine, rockets
200–299 *What men believe in* 　　　(religion)	700–799 *Fine arts* 　　　ex: music, painting
300–399 *How men live together* 　　　(sociology) 　　　ex: UN, government	800–899 *Literature* 　　　ex: poetry
400–499 *Languages* 　　　ex: dictionary	900–999 *History and travel* 　　　ex: biography

The children review the class numbers as in grade three and give examples of books for each class.

Step 2—The children see a filmstrip on the Dewey Decimal System. As each frame appears, the caption is read and discussed.

Step 3—Before working with decimals, the children are reminded that the whole number is of prime importance. On a dittoed list, each child enumerates the whole numbers in order.

352
292
599
612
792
etc.

Then orally they repeat this list of numbers to be shown on the overhead projector. Each child checks his own work against the projected list.

In an alternative drill, an individual Dewey number is given to each child to post in its correct order on the flannelboard.

Step 4—Each two children read a shelf of non-fiction by the whole number only. Then as one reads the whole numbers in order, the other records them. The librarian checks the recorded numbers and if any errors are present, these are discussed before corrections are made on the shelf.

Step 5—The fourth graders are now introduced to the decimal concept. The librarian asks, "Who knows how to write ten cents?"

Although the introduction of decimals may not in many schools coincide with the mathematics program in the elementary school, fourth graders are mature enough to grasp the decimal to second place. The needs of the library program call for the teaching of this concept at this time.

Hence, "Who knows how to write ten cents? twenty-five cents? thirty-six cents?" When each price is mentioned, a child writes it on the board. This is fairly easy of course, but—ah!—five cents, two cents, one cent? These are tricky!

.05	.50	.5
.02	.20	.2
.01	.10	.1

The children are confused with fifty cents, twenty, and ten cents when these are written *without* the zero. There is usually one child in any group, however, who knows how to distinguish between one cent and ten cents (.01 = 1¢ and .1 = 10¢). Willie learns that the zero indicates place when it comes before the number but it stands for nothing when it comes at the end of a decimal . . . so "Why write it?" The children realize then that .1 is still a dime or one-tenth of a dollar.

This concept may be taught by other methods, too, such as illustrating on a board a pie cut in ten parts, or a box of 100 chocolates or a gauge representing one hundred pennies or pieces (Figure 7–1).

In addition, the importance of place in the decimal is clarified by making one decimal exceptionally long in comparison to one that is short but larger, as

$$.25834320928 \ldots \text{ to infinity}$$
$$.32$$
$$.4$$

The children realize through dollars and cents or other media that the .25 is smaller than the .4, that they need not look farther than the first place after the decimal point. It may take two or three lessons to complete the explanation of this concept.

Step 6—The librarian has a list of numbers posted on the board which the class orally arranges in order:

591	591–595–591.5–590–598–612	5 9 0
595		5 9 1
591.5	597.7–512.8–784–553.4–595.4	5 9 1 .5
590		5 9 5
598	780.9–529.1–780–649.5–591.1	5 9 5 .4
612		6 1 2 .8

Having the numbers in a column makes the order obvious. Perhaps one needs to do this before writing the numbers across from left to right as they would normally be on the shelves.

The emphasis is always on the whole number first, with the decimal considered only when the whole numbers differ. Then when two or more whole numbers are the same, the decimal determines which comes next in order. Again, having the children think of the numbers in terms of dollars and cents clarifies any question.

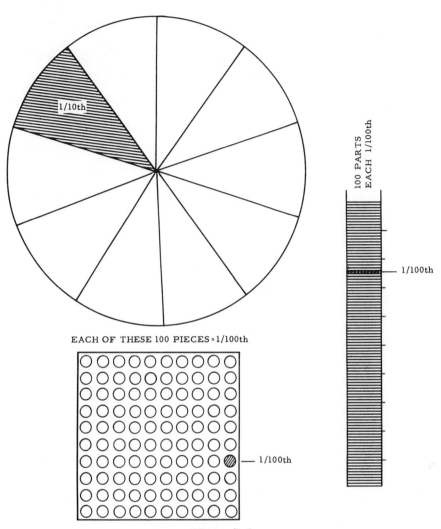

EACH OF THESE 100 PIECES = 1/100th

Figure 7–1.

Step 7— Each child receives a list of eight numbers to enumerate. The librarian and the teacher move from child to child to comment on his grasp of the concept, giving encouragement and individual instruction where necessary. As Debra corrects her errors and receives approval on the first list of classification numbers, she is handed a second list, a little more difficult and with two figures following the decimal point. When II is approved, Debra receives III. Finally for IV she reads a shelf through ten different numbers and records these numbers. A row of books numbered 629.1 would be considered as one number for this activity.

Such a practice may involve two or three library periods.

Dewey Decimal practice: Write the Dewey numbers, smallest on the left to the largest on the right:

I. 973	591.9	591.4	979.4	973.4	591.5
II. 914.38	591.92	595.78	595.7	595	973.4
III. 784.7	973.7	973.6	974.4	973.78	973.28
IV. From the shelf:					

Always the class is reminded that the whole number is of prime importance.

Grade 5

Step 1—Review and practice of the decimal concept as given in grade four occurs again in grade five.

Step 2—The Cutter-Sanborn[2] letter is introduced:

520	520		629.1	629.1
H	G		L	B

Which comes first in each set?

Each fifth grader now receives a packet of thirty different call numbers which he manipulates until the numbers are in order.

595.78	560	745.5	353.45	595.4	595.4
C	G	S	C	M	B

Of course the children need plenty of elbow room and table space for this exercise and guidance from the librarian and the classroom

---

[2] In schools that meet American Library Association standards, one may want to introduce the Cutter-Sanborn numbers before the decimals in Dewey since the number following the author letter is a decimal, although the decimal point is not printed; e.g.,

    Gag   G132   The 132 is treated as a decimal.
    Kipling   K57   The 57 is treated as a decimal.

From here one moves to the decimals in the Dewey Decimal classification. In many schools, however, where money and personnel are short, only the Cutter-Sanborn letter is given with the classification number.

teacher. As each child completes his set of cards and individual questions have been answered, the child shuffles the cards in his packet and rubberbands them again so they are ready for another group.

Step 3—Each fifth grader again receives one packet of call number practice cards. After these are arranged in order, he is given the second packet to interfile with it. A third packet for interfiling may be added.

Step 4—When the class has mastered the order of the classification numbers, every two children are assigned a shelf to read with at least ten different classification numbers. The librarian may have posted on the chalkboard the sections or divisions from which the children may make their choices:

```
John and Gary  ........ 507–537
Mary and Sue   ........ 549–560
Willie and Debra ...... 600–624
                        636–688
                        800–812
                        900–915 etc.
```

The books assigned may also be on the book cart. Or, in smaller libraries sets of books are placed between bookends on the tables for the overflow of pupils and to avoid crowding at the shelves. Even a stack of book jackets properly numbered may be used.

After the books are in order, one child states the numbers while the other records them in that same order. They double check the list and make necessary changes on it before correcting the order of the books on the shelf. A quick glance across the list of numbers tells the librarian whether the books are being read properly. This solves the problem, too, of how the librarian may check individual shelf work if she is pressed for time. Each child also becomes more aware of whether he is reading the shelf correctly when he sees his "answers" in print.

Step 5—Another method used extensively is to have each child read a whole shelf himself. Willie reshelves the misshelved books correctly. He leaves such books jutting half way out for the librarian to check. (See Figure 7–2.)

The amount of practice and individual help will depend on the length of the library period and the professional personnel available.

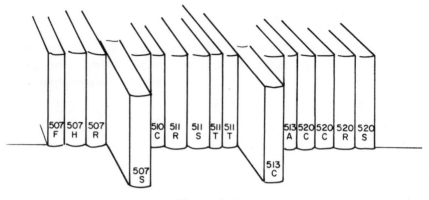

Figure 7–2.

Step 6—In addition to reading a shelf, Willie shelves a dozen books from the cart, shelving the books only half way in or identifying them with colored strips of paper so the librarian may spot, check, and align them with the shelf when they are correct. When errors occur, the librarian gives individual guidance.

In this unit on reading the shelves, the librarian needs frequently to emphasize that the classification numbers are of prime concern. The Cutter-Sanborn letters are considered only when the classification numbers are the same:

559	560	560	560	571
D	A	P	Z	B

This concept cannot be stressed too much as the librarian, otherwise, finds to her horror that several children are shelving the books perfectly according to the alphabet! Experience is a wise teacher.

For further practice and application, the children take turns enumerating the daily non-fiction circulation or checking-in books. Now the relationship between the order of the book cards and the arrangement of books on the shelves comes to light.

Step 7—Before leaving Mr. Dewey, the fifth graders learn that biography is the exception to the rule. Up to this time they have known the Cutter-Sanborn letter represents the author. But here's a book by Judson:

921	George Washington
W	

The W obviously does not stand for the author's name as one would normally expect. Through inquiry from the librarian, the children realize the W is for Washington because the book is all about Washington. In like manner

$$\boxed{\begin{array}{c} 921 \\ \mathrm{L} \end{array}}$$

The L stands for books on Lincoln or other persons whose names begin with L. The class begins to understand that the reason for the Cutter-Sanborn letter representing, not the author, but the biographee is that all the books about one person will be together on the shelf. Use of the Cutter-Sanborn number with the letter leaves no doubt of this.

In oral practice, each one names a famous person of his choice and gives the classification number and Cutter-Sanborn letter.

Step 8—The children receive a list representing biographies in their library. They underline that part of the title that the Cutter-Sanborn letter stands for, such as:

Martin <u>Luther</u> for $\boxed{\begin{array}{c} 921 \\ \mathbf{L} \end{array}}$

In instances where the name does not appear in the title, the children check for the book on the shelf. The annotation on the catalog card or in H. W. Wilson's *Children's Catalog* often reveals the biographee. The children write in the name, such as:

<u>Chapman</u> for $\boxed{\begin{array}{c} 921 \\ \mathrm{C} \end{array}}$ *Better Known as Johnny Appleseed*

PRACTICE IN SHELVING BIOGRAPHY

Underline or write in the biographee:

921		921	
A	Jane Addams	C	Voyages of Christopher Columbus
	Ah-yo-ka, Daughter of Sequoia		
921		921	
B	Carry On, Mr. Bowditch	D	Virginia Dare
	The First Woman Doctor	921	
	. . . .	E	Queen Elizabeth
	Seeing Fingers	921	
921		G	Vasco da Gama
C	Buffalo Bill	921	
		J	Joan of Arc
			John Paul Jones

Grade 6

*Steps 1 and 2—*The sixth graders need a good review:

a. Orally via the chalkboard or overhead projector
b. Written list to be put in order
c. Reading shelves and listing the numbers from these as in the fifth grade

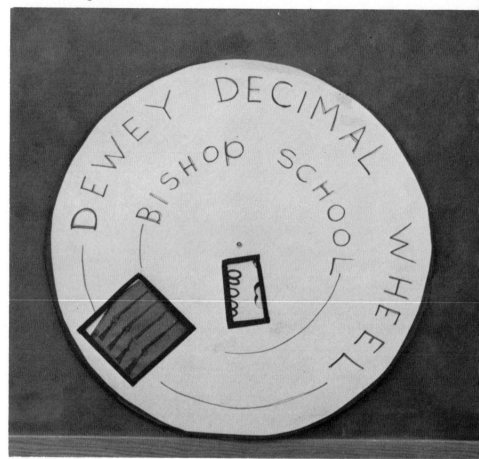

Figure 7–3.

*Step 3—*The Dewey Decimal wheel may be used effectively in grade six for variety. (See Figures 7–3 and 14–1.) The inner wheel is spun until it stops at a picture or a Dewey number in a window of the wheel. Each child may take a turn at spinning the wheel and identifying a picture or subject by Dewey number, or naming the subject for the Dewey number revealed in the window. The wheel is available for children to use during browsing periods.

Step 4—A drill which can be done, after an initial discussion of Dewey, is to give a number of small committees a list of non-fiction titles to which Dewey numbers are to be assigned. The members of each group discuss the possibilities. There is often a difference of opinion. At this stage, titles which have clues to the subjects need to be used:

> *Grimm's Fairy Tales*
> *Prehistoric Animals*
> *The First Book of Airplanes*
> *The Big Book of Trains*
> *The Golden Book of Poetry*

A final summing up of the unit on the Dewey Decimal system is the puzzle story *Mr. Dewey's Naughty Boy*. This is appropriate for the fifth graders as well as the sixth. The children write above each number the subject it represents. In each case it should, of course, make sense.

MR. DEWEY'S NAUGHTY BOY

700's real name was Arthur, after the king in 398, but to his friends he was 700. He wasn't really a bad boy when on his own. He didn't steal 332.4. He never scuffed his 685.3 because he was too lazy to scramble over 552 and 582.17. Experimenting with 540, playing 796.357, going 797.2, or watching 621.388 were his ideas of fun.

But 423 was not his favorite indoor 796! He literally hated 513 and tried to escape it in every conceivable way. Once with a 737 he short-circuited all the 537 in the 513 classroom on a rainy day.

One day after school his mother said: "Come, 700, I don't want to 947, but it's time for you to practice your 786.2. You can't spend all day making model 629.14."

"Oh, Mom," said 700, "skip the 371.33. I wish I'd been born in 972 where they aren't in such a rush. Even an 970.1 has more 790 than I do. Mike's mother doesn't ask him to do anything. She doesn't care how much he 812."

"Never mind, my 523. Come right in here. It's time for you to 910.

Don't slam that door! Don't go bumping that 749. That 666.1 is my best 951, and oh, you've broken it! You do have the awfullest 395! A 636.2 in the house couldn't be worse. If anybody ever writes my 921, it will say I died young on account of my 364.36."

She didn't, however, and 700 finally became a man, and now the whole thing is 930.

Each one tries to locate all the answers. But, to avoid everyone's crowding the shelves for the same number, the class may be divided so each group starts at a different paragraph and may continue to the end, then back up to paragraph 1, etc.

After the class has spent a reasonable time locating the answers on the shelves, the story is read aloud, the subject being stated in place of each number. For various reasons, some numbers may not be represented on the shelves. Here is a natural opportunity for introducing the reference tools: Dewey's *Decimal Classification* and the *Children's Catalog*.

From this point on, the children should feel at home at the non-fiction shelves. The library is beginning to be second nature to many of them; and for these, perhaps, this is a major step toward a lifetime library habit.

Chapter 8—

The Card Catalog—

Making the Card Catalog

Easy

Children are great imitators and followers. The cluster of boys and girls around the card catalog fascinates the uninitiated. Debra simply has to get her fingers into those drawers. She peers into drawer after drawer, flipping the cards busily back and forth (Figure 8–1).

"Debra, do you need help?" asks the librarian.

Figure 8–1.

"Well, no, not exactly. I'm trying to find a book on dogs." Debra is only one of many third graders anxious to use the card catalog.

Now Willie presents a different problem from Debra. His interest in camping leads him innocently to yank out of the drawer a pack of subject cards on camping, stuffing them into his pocket. The inevitable happens, of course; someone tells! When the cards are retrieved, Willie confides to the librarian that he thought he could learn how to camp by studying the cards—he is far ahead of his class on automation in the library!

It is obvious that Willie and his classmates need to—and are ready to—learn about the card catalog. Their training thus far has prepared them for it.

1. The twenty-six letters
2. The Easy books and their arrangement
3. Alphabetical order of authors, titles, and subjects.

Grade 3

Step 1—Before starting actual work on the card catalog, the librarian points out that it is made up of many drawers which are kept in alphabetical order and that each drawer has a label on the front telling which cards are kept in that drawer. (See Figure 8–2.) She pulls out a drawer to show the class it contains many cards. The librarian confronted with a Willie problem, or with children who ask questions about the locking rod may, at this moment, turn the drawer upside down to show the class that the cards will not fall out. She strongly emphasizes that *never,* in any library, does a patron re-

Figure 8–2.

A	B	C	D-E	F
G	H	I-K	L-M	N-O
P-R	S	T	U-V	W-Z

move cards from the card catalog. Most children will reason out the various answers for this.

In introducing the contents of the card catalog the librarian first talks about an object familiar to many children: the mail order catalog. Children may be asked to bring a catalog from home to share with the class.

When curiosity about the catalog is satisfied the librarian raises the following points:

Mail Order Catalog	*Card Catalog*
1. Items are pictured and numbered.	1. Books are identified and call numbered.
2. The index gives a quick rundown on what items are included in the catalog—and storehouse.	2. One or more cards for each book indicate which books the library owns.
3. The index is in alphabetical order.	3. The card catalog is in alphabetical order.
4. Numbers are *not* in 1–2–3 order but they are in boldface type.	4. Numbers are not in order but they are prominently located on the card.

Step 2— The third graders learn that the card catalog identifies each book in the library collection by author. To clarify this

Figure 8–3.

point two children stand in front of the class. As illustrated in Figure 8–3, one child holds up a book so the front cover may be clearly seen. A second child holds the large sample author card for this book. The librarian asks questions whose answers point out the relationship between the book and the card. E.g., as she points to the author on the author card, she asks:

1. What does this have to do with the book?
2. What part of the name comes first?
3. Why does this name come first?
4. What punctuation mark is used on the card after the author's last name?
5. On what line of the card is the author's name?

Step 3—Again two children stand before the class, one holding the same book, the other the same author card. The children briefly review the points covered in Step 2. Then the librarian paperclips above the author's name a strip containing the title (Figure 8–4). She asks:

1. What is the top line now?
2. Where else on the card does this appear?
3. How many times does the title appear on the title card?
4. Where is the title located?
5. Where does the title start in relation to the author's name? (The word "indent" is introduced here.)

Figure 8–4.

6. Now the librarian changes the card back to an author card and asks, "What kind of a card did we have to start with?" After the children reply, she again holds the title strip above the author's name and asks, "Now what kind of a card is that?"

The librarian removes the title strip and another child holds the author card. The librarian asks the class, "What do you think is the subject of this book?"

When the correct subject is decided upon, she adds the subject strip to the card.

1. What kind of a card is it now?
2. How does the top line look different?
3. Where does the subject start in relation to the author's name?

In conclusion, the three types of cards are displayed side by side, with a quick review of the significance of the top line on each card.

Step 4—The children's attention is drawn to the call number on a large sample card and they are reminded that in the mail order catalog the number beside the item indicates the location of the item in the warehouse. The librarian now shows them, by walking to the shelves, that the call number shows the book's location in the library. In their earlier lessons about the Cutter-Sanborn letters on the book spine, the children became familiar with the term "call number," the address of the book.

To continue the comparison with the familiar, a mail order catalog, the librarian asks, "How does the mail order catalog get to Debra's house?" Most third graders know it is through the address on the wrapping. Debra is asked to step to the chalkboard and in a previously drawn square place the following name and address:

```
Debra Green
636 G Street
```

Beside this the librarian places an example of a catalog card:

```
636
G     Green, Debra
```

She emphasizes that the address of the book is always the call number and is always in the upper lefthand corner of the catalog card.[1]

*Step 5—*The next point taken up is the arrangement of the cards in the card catalog. When asked, many children may reply, "By call number!" The range of answers even includes the copyright date. When the librarian introduces the word "alphabetical" and asks for its meaning, every hand in the room waves madly. *Everyone* knows that! Hasn't the class put authors, titles, and subjects into alphabetical order all fall? The librarian agrees that this is what has been done on the chalkboard, but how about the card catalog itself?

> Debra thinks by author.
> Willie thinks by title.
> Another child ventures, "By subject."

The children cannot reach an agreement.

The librarian brings out the giant tagboard cards and reminds the children of the author's inverted name and the rule for ignoring "A," "An," and "The" when they appear first in titles. The class knows by now the way in which the subject is indicated. Libraries vary in their use of capital letters, red type, or underlining.

As each author card is displayed, the children are asked: "What appears on the top line?" When the title card is displayed, the children are asked the same question: "What appears on the top line?" Then the subject card is displayed with the same question. Thus the children realize that the three previous answers were all correct concerning the alphabetizing of catalog cards, and when the final question is asked: "The cards, whether author, title, or subject, are arranged alphabetically by what on the card?" the class shouts

"THE TOP LINE!"

The sample cards are now lined up alphabetically according to the top line.[2]

*Step 6—*The class arrives to find catalog trays on the tables. Two children share a tray (Figure 8–5). The librarian instructs them, "Find five different cards with the author's name on the top line." One child searches while the other records. Five subject cards are then located and noted down, the children changing roles. And finally five titles are listed.

---

1 This step is extended in detail in Chapter 7.
2 This, of course, applies to libraries using a dictionary-type catalog.

Figure 8–5.

In an alternative drill, the librarian instructs, "Find a card with the author's name on the top line." She and the teacher move about, checking to see that the children are actually locating author cards. The librarian asks each one to

1. Name the author on the card.
2. State which part of the author's name comes first. *Last.*
3. State where the author's name occurs on the card. *Top line.*

Each third grader now looks for the title of a book on the top line. Now the librarian asks:

1. What is on the top line? *The title.*
2. How many times does the title appear on the card? *Twice.*
3. Where does the title appear? *Above and below the author's name.*

E	The Runaway Bunny
B	Brown, Margaret Wise.
	The Runaway Bunny, illustrated by Clement Hurd.
	Harper, 1942.
	unp. illus.

Last, a subject card is located and described.

1. Where is the subject located? *Top line.*
2. How do you know it's the subject? *All capital letters.*

```
E        RABBITS—FICTION
B        Brown, Margaret Wise.
         The Runaway Bunny, illustrated by Clement Hurd.
         Harper, 1942.
         unp. illus.
```

Grade 4

Step 1—With the giant tagboard cards before them, the fourth graders review the three types of cards: author, title, subject,—and the call number. Each has a turn identifying the card displayed or answering a question pertaining to it. These are lined up in alphabetical order by the first line.

The librarian queries:

1. If you have read a very good book and want to read more books by the same author, what kind of a card do you look for?
2. If you remember the title of a book but have forgotten the author's name, how can you find out who wrote the book?
3. Willie wants a book on snakes but doesn't know the title or author of such a book. How does he find them?
4. What can be learned from the call number on the card?

Step 2—The fourth graders progress to other information on the card: publisher, illustrator, copyright,[3] and number of pages. The class discusses each item:

1. The author is the person who writes the book.
2. The publisher is the company that prints the book.
3. The illustrator is the artist, the person who draws the pictures.

NOTE: By looking at a catalog card, one can tell whether the book has pictures because the abbreviation *illus.* will appear after the number of pages (ie., the collation) .

A simple beginning drill is to have the class name the various parts of the card. The librarian points to these, but not necessarily in order. The last time around, the parts are named in order. As the

---

[3] Copyright information is presented in detail in Chapter 5.

children name the various parts of the author card for the last time, one child posts these on the chalkboard for those unfamiliar with the spelling.

As sample cards are held up, the children may take turns answering the following questions:

1. What is the author's name?
2. How many pages does the book have?
3. Does the book have pictures?
4. What is the publisher's name?
5. What year was the book copyrighted?
6. What is the title of the book?

Each child receives a dittoed author card as illustrated in Figure 8–6. On this he identifies the parts, which meanwhile have been erased from the chalkboard. These are checked by the librarian and returned at the next visit of the class.

Figure 8–6.

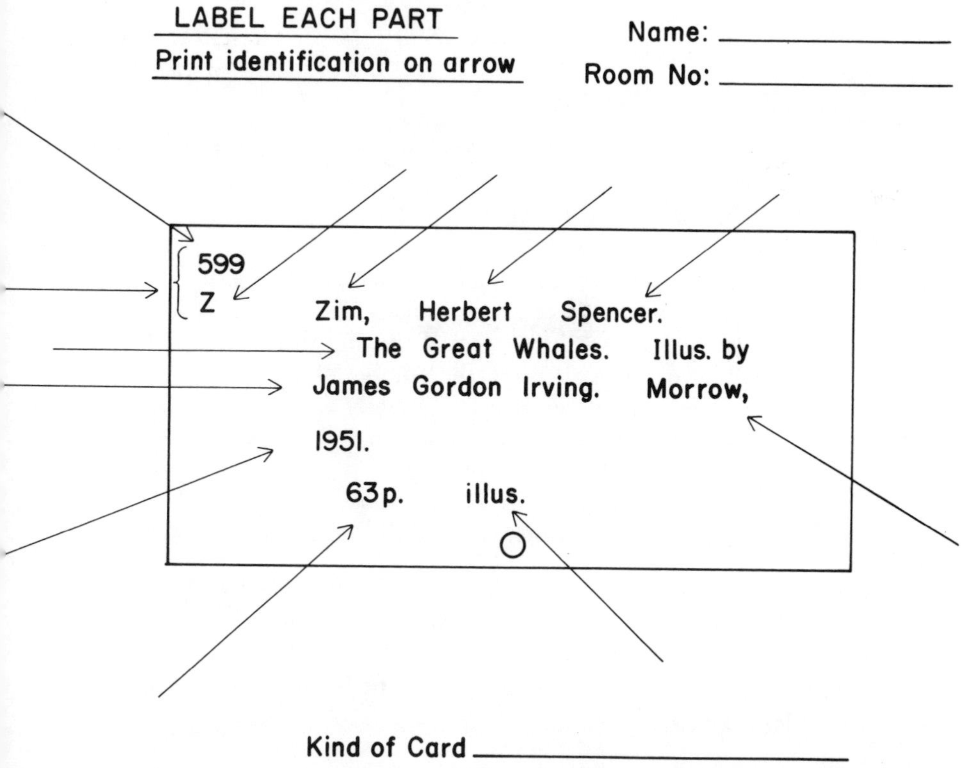

LABEL EACH PART

Print identification on arrow

Name: _____

Room No: _____

599
Z

Zim, Herbert Spencer.
The Great Whales. Illus. by
James Gordon Irving. Morrow,
1951.
63p. illus.
O

Kind of Card _____

Step 3—On the lower part of a flannelboard are all the parts of an author card, purposely mixed up. Members of the class take turns assembling the author card, placing the parts in correct order. Each one adds one part.

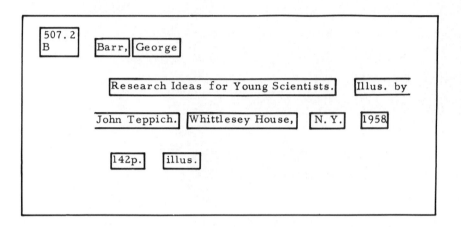

It is best to have a title long enough to extend the paragraph into a second line.

The librarian then asks:

1. Where does the author's name begin in relation to the call number?
2. Where does the title begin?
3. How do you know this is a paragraph?
4. Where does the second line of the paragraph begin?
5. What begins the next paragraph?
6. What is the difference between putting the letter "p" *before* the number of pages and *after* the number of pages?
7. How many paragraphs occur directly under the author's name?
8. What word begins the first paragraph?
9. . . . the second paragraph?
10. What is another word for *illustrations*?
11. How can you tell which is the author and which the publisher?

Of course these questions are based on a catalog card with only the basic information to avoid confusing the child (Figures 8–7 and 8–8). Manipulating these strips, with critical classmates looking on, helps fix the material and its arrangement firmly in the child's mind. (See Figures 8–9, 8–10, and 8–11.)

Figure 8–7.

Figure 8–8.

Figure 8–9.

Figure 8–10.

Figure 8–11.

Step 4—The fourth graders again build an author card of tagboard strips on the flannelboard. One child changes the author card to a title card. Another changes it to a subject card.

Then follows a comparison of the information on the three types of sample cards, simultaneously displayed. The conclusion is that all three cards from the author's name through the collation are exactly the same except for an additional title line above the author's name for the title card; or, the subject line above the author's name for a subject card.

The children complete the unit by copying their dittoed author card twice (without the identifications). After these are copied exactly, each child turns one into a title card and the other into a subject card.

Grade 5

Step 1—Grade five reviews the lessons on the card catalog early in the year. A repetition of simple drills such as those with the flannelboard in the fourth grade help recall the material to the child's mind.

   Step 2—The librarian places a stack of books on each table, one for each child. Possibly the class may browse first and each one will work with the book he has just checked out. Each pupil receives four clean 3x5 cards on which to make one author, one title, and one subject card for the same book. The author card is checked for accuracy before the child is asked to copy it twice. He repeats the title for a title card on one slip, and states the subject on the other for a subject card.

   Each child alphabetizes his three cards and adds the fourth card, with his name on it, to the top of the pack.

   Step 3—Each child is handed back his pack of three cards. After he checks these for alphabetical order, he and his neighbor interfile their six cards together. Then all the children at one table arrange their cards alphabetically as in a regular card catalog. All through this procedure the cards are placed on the table with just the first two lines showing.

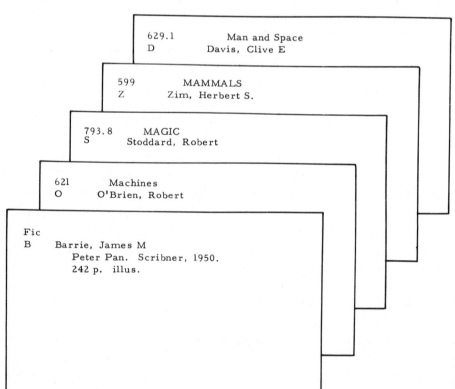

Often there are several children who wish to pursue this further. They may interfile all these practice cards in a box.

Step 4—If further practice is needed, each fifth grader may receive a pack of twelve sample catalog cards numbered one to twelve on the back. Each one files his pack in alphabetical order. When the filing is correct, the pupil identifies the information on each card as follows:

Card	Kind of Card	Call No.	Author	No. Pp.	Publ.
Example	Author	Fic B	James Barrie	235	Grosset
1					
2					
3 etc.					

Grade 6

Step 1—If there is need the sixth graders have a brief review of the above material, followed by the introduction of cross reference cards, again demonstrated with the tagboard cards: both "see" and "see also" cards are shown. An analytic card is also discussed at this time if this type of card appears in the card catalog. (See Figure 8–12.)

The explanation of these cards may be very brief: a cross reference card *refers* the patron from one subject *across* to another; an analytic card *analyzes* the subjects in a book that are not taken care of by the subject card.

Also discussed at this time may be cards in the card catalog for pictures, pamphlets, records, and filmstrips if any or all of these are present in the card catalog. The children need to know by what means such materials are indicated in their card catalog.

Step 2—The major portion of instruction on the card catalog for sixth graders is the filing of the cards in the card catalog. The children go over the filing rules:

1. Alphabetize by the top line.
2. Ignore *A, An, The* when they begin a title.
3. Spell out all numbers and abbreviations.
4. Place shorter words before longer ones: "With the zebras" comes before "Without apples."

```
TADPOLES

                    See

               FROGS
               TOADS




                     O
```
Cross Reference

```
               AERONAUTICS

                 See also

          AERONAUTICS--FLIGHTS
          AERONAUTICS--MILITARY
          AIR PILOTS
          AIRPLANES
          BALLOONS
          HELICOPTERS
          PARACHUTES

                     O
```
Cross Reference

```
910        Cabot, John, p. 47-53
L      Lambert, R        S
           The World's Most Daring Explorers.
       Sterling, 1956.

       Analytic Card




                     O
```
Analytic Card

Figure 8–12.

The children pair off to (1) read the card catalog trays and (2) do preliminary filing of the cards for new books that have been processed.

In reading the trays, each two children read for errors. The librarian places colored strips of paper on each table. The children sign one colored strip and place it vertically in the front of the tray. When, and if, they find an error, they place a strip of colored paper in front of the misfiled card so the strip sticks up like a periscope. The librarian moves about the room and checks the "findings" in each tray. Very often she needs to explain why the "correction" is not an error. Examples of filing apt to be considered errors:

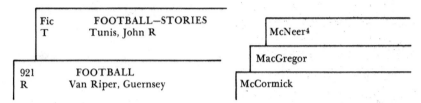

Fic	FOOTBALL—STORIES		McNeer[4]
T	Tunis, John R		
			MacGregor
921	FOOTBALL		
R	Van Riper, Guernsey		McCormick

Or if it shows an actual error, she compliments the children and has them indicate where the card ought to be filed. Children whose findings were all correct have the strip in the front of the tray marked with an "A" or some other notation. The librarian refiles correctly erroneously placed cards.

Step 3—For the strips pertaining to cards that the children erroneously thought were misfiled, the librarian makes a record of the cards involving each instance. The librarian lists these "errors" on the overhead projector or the chalkboard. The class indicates the filing rule which pertains to each one of these. This is preparation for the last lesson in filing.

Step 4—Children feel it is quite a privilege to do actual filing in the card catalog. And they become very much aware of new titles available. As they do the PRELIMINARY filing, two children to a tray, the librarian gives individual guidance. After the class leaves, she makes a final check of their above-the-rod filing before dropping the cards into the trays.

Drill in the card catalog becomes meaningful as committees work on bibliographies for sixth grade units of study in science and social studies, compiling lists of books directly from the card catalog. The lists are divided into fiction and non-fiction; the author, title, and call number for each one are listed. The bibliographies may then be posted in the sixth grade classrooms, with copies available in the library.

---

4 "Mc" is an abbreviation of "Mac."

Chapter 9—

Rocketing into Reference—

How to Use Reference

Books

"Teacher, Springfield isn't here. I've looked all over the map for it," complains Willie . . . "Did you check the map key?" asks the librarian . . . "Map key?" . . . "Yes, the key given in the index," answers the librarian. "Here, let me show you." And Willie is given a personal lesson in locating places on the map.

MAPS[1]

Although teaching the reading of maps is usually a classroom activity, the library often reinforces it. It is necessary for the class to practice such learning with a wall map before beginning a unit on atlases and gazetteers, for the learning here will be related to the maps in atlases and other types of books. Such lessons may start as early as the second grade.

Grade 2

Step 1—Early in grade two, the librarian presents several

---

[1] The Education or Public Relations divisions of the large oil companies will furnish maps upon request. It is possible to obtain enough duplicate maps so each pupil in the class has one to work from. With these maps open before them, the children practice locating various places, either from a list on the chalkboard or from names with their key locations suggested by members of the class. This type of map work is suitable for use with older groups.

lessons on locating places on a large political wall map of the United States. Broad horizontal and vertical lines are made on the map. The sections are marked A B C . . . across the top, and numbered along the side so the letters and numbers are plainly visible across the room. Second graders are capable of running a ruler from A to A across a map, and from 1 to 1 down a map. They can then easily see where the lines intersect. This is the first step in learning how to locate places on a map.

The librarian points out how rivers, lakes, oceans, mountains, and cities are indicated.

She then quizzes the second graders on such locations as

North, East, South, West	Pacific Ocean
United States	Great Lakes
Canada	Mississippi River
Mexico	State in which the children live
Atlantic Ocean	City where school is located

This can be an expansion of classroom lessons on streets and places in the immediate locale. The library instruction may very well give second graders their first awareness of the boundaries of the United States.

Step 2—The material in step one is reviewed and after the class has its bearings in this respect, the librarian asks each one who came from a different state to point it out.

Step 3—This next step has been tried successfully with second graders. However, the librarian will want to let the teacher decide whether this step could better wait till the class reaches third grade. If so, then it would precede step 1 on that level.

The librarian explains the significance of the lines, the letters across the top indicating the *vertical* areas (those which run up and down), and the numbers along the side indicating the *horizontal* (those which run across). Second graders can learn both in the library and in the classroom that the word *horizontal* is related to the *horizon*. They are very much aware of sunsets; so, to point out that the line at which the earth and the sky meet is the *horizon* readily conveys the idea.

When the children understand these, the librarian illustrates how to locate particular places on the map according to the key, such as San Francisco: A–3. Two pointers or yardsticks are used to indicate that the square which they intersect contains a specific location. Various members of the class locate significant places or names in the national news, using the key:

Cape Kennedy	New York City
Dallas, Texas	Chicago, Illinois
Washington, D.C.	Capital of state in which the children live

Several names whose locations are unfamiliar test whether the children understand the concept of locating places on the map.

Going beyond the continental United States, the children point out Honolulu, Hawaii; Cuba; Guadalajara, Mexico; Victoria, B.C.

Grade 3

The above activities may be started in grade three if they are not presented in grade two; or, they can be further extended here. The use of dittoed maps may give each one the experience of reading maps. Books on geography and travel have high interest level at this time.

Step 1—The material covered in grade two will need to be reviewed. With that, the children may learn the new words: *longitude,* the vertical lines; and *latitude,* the horizontal lines. They may indicate these when locating places on the map.

Step 2—The political map that was used for grade two hangs on the wall. Each child is given a dittoed map of the United States. An accompanying worksheet tells the children what to do. This could nicely be a follow-up lesson in the classroom. To accomplish it, children will need crayons.

1. Mark North, East, South, West on the map
2. Color the oceans blue
3. Color the lakes green
4. Color the state in which you live red
5. Make a star for the city where you live

In cooperation with the classroom teacher a model map may be made. This might be a map of the city where the school is located or an imaginary city. Schools, churches, markets, hospitals, railroad lines, major roads, housing developments, etc. may be indicated in various ways. This gives the children practical experience in pinpointing exact locations and in working with a legend. Displayed in the library, model maps attract the attention of children at all grade levels.

Grade 4

Step 1—Fourth graders are ready for the map series. The collection of charts on reading map symbols[2] gives explanations and illustrated example questions. The five charts are as follows:

Small signs on a map stand for big things on the earth

Example: ⭘ = town 〰〰 = road

How we show on a map some things made by nature

Example: ⠿ = large dots stand for gravelly deserts

How we show on a map some things made by people

Example: ⌒⌒ = railroads ≈≈≈ = canals

How transportation routes are shown on a map

Example: ⬡51 = highways ——— = airplane routes

How we show the surface of the earth on a map

Example: │orange│ = mountains │green│ = lowlands

---

2 This material is taken from *Map Symbols and Geographic Terms* by Zoe A. Thralls and Frances M. Hanson. Chart courtesy A. J. Nystrom & Co., Chicago 60618.

MAPS AND GAZETTEERS

Step 2—The librarian and the children first define

An atlas: A bound volume of maps
A gazetteer: A dictionary of geographical names

The librarian displays the various atlases in the library and points out the main features of each. Similar sections in the encyclopedia are examined. Several samples of index references posted on the chalkboard or projected on a screen help to explain the use of map references. E.g., from the *Britannica World Atlas:*

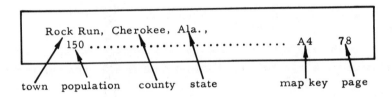

Rock Run, Cherokee, Ala., 150 . . . . A4 78

town   population   county   state   map key   page

Step 3—The fourth graders, in pairs, receive cards with questions whose answers they locate in the atlases available. These will need to be very simple to encourage the children in their understanding of reading maps. Examples are given in the following:

GLOBAL ATLAS
Name five types of transportation in the United States pictured on the pictorial map of North America.

BRITANNICA WORLD ATLAS
1. Through what states does the Missouri River flow?
2. What states border Illinois?

WEBSTER'S GEOGRAPHICAL DICTIONARY
1. What is the area of Denmark?
2. Where is the Bay of Campeche?

Grade 5

ATLASES AND GAZETTEERS

Step 1—An intensive lesson as indicated in the map series above is repeated for fifth graders on the meanings of map symbols.

Step 2—A filmstrip on maps, atlases, and gazetteers prepares the class for lessons in

1. *Britannica World Atlas*
2. *Historical Atlas of the United States*
3. *American History Atlas*
4. *Global Atlas*
5. *Hammond's Nature Atlas of America*
6. *Webster's Geographical Dictionary*
7. Maps in encyclopedias

Step 3—On the board are posted samples from the indexes of several atlases to show the variations among them (Figure 9–1).

Figure 9–1.

Name of Atlas	City	Country	Page or Plate No.
Hammond's Advanced Reference Atlas	Roma (capital)	Italy	25
Hammond's Historical Atlas	Rome (Roma)		H - 6
Hammond's Standard World Atlas	Roma (Rome)	Italy	18
Goode's World Atlas	Roma (Rome) (ró ma) (rom)	It.	
Britannica World Atlas	Rome (Roma)	It.	21

Through inquiry, the librarian draws from the class the significance of the letters and numbers given in these references. An overhead projector may be used for the same purpose.

    Step 4—Atlases and gazetteers are distributed to such fifth grade classes as are academically ready for this exercise. Each panel of three or four children browse through and prepare a critical review of just what their reference book contains, such as the following:

1. A political map, showing man-made features, e.g., boundaries between countries
2. A physical map, showing features made by nature, e.g., mountains
3. A pictorial map, where the information is given through drawings, e.g., products of a state
4. A gazetteer, a list of various geographical locations with a description of each
5. Tables of facts and figures (Figure 9–2). *Britannica World Atlas,* for example, has an extensive section of geographical summaries and comparisons.

Square Miles	Population	Index Reference	Region	Latitude	Longitude
116,000	45,600,000 (country)	K 7			
		D - 4			
	1,610,467 (city)	D 4			
			Rome In.	41-52N	12:37 E
	1,750,700 (city)	D4, L8			

Figure 9-2.

Bahama Islands

Bahamas 3 Population of cities

City1	1953 census	1958 estimate
Nassau*, New Providence	46,125	50,405

1 Municipality.

Bahamas 5 Number of livestock

Type	1950 estimate	1959 estimate
Cattle	3,800	3,600
Goats	14,000	14,000
Horses	3,500	3,600
Poultry	385,000	408,000
Sheep	22,600	22,600
Swine	7,800	10,200

Bahamas 8 Sea products

Product	1950 Amount tons	1950 U.S. dollars	1959ᵃ Amount tons	1959ᵃ U.S. dollars
TOTAL	...			653,547
Crayfish	1,522	164,312	1,197	636,966
Scalefish	151	10,704	0.5	67
Sponge	62	10,069	3	16,514
Turtle	57	8,697	—	—
Others	...		—	—

ᵃ Exports only.

Bahamas 1 Area and population

Political subdivision	Area Square miles	Population 1953 census Urban	% of total	Rural	Total	Density per sq.mi.	Population 1955 estimate Total	Density per sq.mi.
TOTAL	4,404	...	...	...	84,841	19.3	87,702	19.9
DISTRICTS								
Abaco and Cays	776	...	...	...	3,407	4.4	3,540	4.6
Acklins Island	120	...	...	...	1,273	10.6	2,294ᵃ	...
Andros Island	1,600	...	...	...	7,136	4.5	7,852	4.9
Berry Islands	14	...	...	...	327	23.4	247	17.6
Biminis	9	...	...	...	1,325	147.2	1,222	135.8
Cat Island	160	...	...	...	3,201	20.0	3,320	20.8
Cay Lobos	7	...	...	...	5	0.7	...	...
Crooked Island	76	...	...	...	836	11.0	2,294ᵃ	...
Eleuthera	164	...	...	...	6,070	37.0	5,386	32.8
Exuma and Cays	100	...	...	...	2,919	29.2	2,700	27.0
Grand Bahama	430	...	...	...	4,095	9.5	4,600	10.7
Harbour Island	1.5	...	...	...	840	560.0	2,094	1,396.0
Inagua	560	...	...	...	999	1.8	1,040	1.9
Long Cay	8	...	...	...	80	10.0	2,294ᵃ	...
Long Island	130	...	...	...	3,755	28.9	3,869	29.8
Mayaguana	96	...	...	...	615	6.4	546	5.7
New Providence	58	...	...	...	46,125	795.3	46,920	809.0
Ragged Island and Cays	5	...	...	...	320	64.0	347	69.4
Rum Cay	29	...	...	...	133	4.6	129	4.4
San Salvador (Watlings Island)	60	...	...	...	694	11.6	906	15.1
Spanish Wells	0.5	...	...	...	686	1,372.0	690	1,380.0

Bahamas 7 Forest products

Product	1950[a]		1959[a]	
	Amount	U.S. dollars	Amount	U.S. dollars
TOTAL	...	...	...	2,646,876
Cascarilla bark	12 tons	3,318	12 tons	5,289
Mine props			—	60,586
Pine lumber	8,142,000 bd. ft.	677,152	587,000 bd. ft.	2,574,681[b]
Other lumber	114 tons	4,362	231[b] tons	6,320
Others	...	...	115 "	...

[a] *Exports only.* [b] *Pulpwood.*

Bahamas 9 Manufacturing

Manufactural group	1950			1959		
	Number of establishments	Number of workers	U.S. dollars	Number of establishments	Number of workers	U.S. dollars
TOTAL	...	...	...	...	...	240,000
Canning (tomatoes, pineapple)	3			4		
Lumber	2			2		
Shoes	1			...		
Woodworking	...			3		
Miscellaneous	...			...		

(Left-hand portion, partially cut off at binding)

%	1959 Amount	U.S. dollars
	30,000 cu. yd.	65,000
	4,620 tons	
	67,000 "	210,000
	170,400 cu. yd.	773,392
	3,290 tons	87,172
	232,400 "	766,920

%	1957 U.S. dollars	%	1959 U.S. dollars	%
100.0	46,590,289	100.0	75,582,458	100.0
	42,735,073	100.0	69,566,535	100.0
38.6	22,034,874	51.5	39,279,355	56.5
28.5	9,595,807	22.5	18,569,914	26.7
12.2	3,066,185	7.2	3,432,596	4.9
4.9	92,103	0.2	89,046	0.1
4.4	2,284,206	5.3	2,531,267	3.6
0.7	279,927	0.7	425,326	0.6
10.7	5,381,971	12.6	5,239,031	7.5
100.0	3,855,216	100.0	6,015,923	100.0
33.5	3,095,682	80.3	5,532,772	91.9
20.4	231,787	6.0	257,897	4.3
14.6	123,273	3.2	95,748	1.6
4.6	—		—	
4.6	12,919	0.3	16,803	0.3
22.3	391,555	10.2	112,703	1.9

Figure 9–2 (continued).

A. Summaries on the world and individual countries, including:
   a. Area and population
   b. Population by groups
   c. Population of cities
   d. Crop production
   e. Number of livestock
   f. Mineral production
   g. Forest products
   h. Sea products
   i. Manufacturing
   j. Value of foreign trade
   k. Exports
   l. Imports.
B. Geographical comparisons:
   a. Waterfalls
   b. Oceans and seas
   c. Principal islands
   d. Largest lakes
   e. Longest rivers
   f. Mountain peaks
   g. Famous ship canals
   h. Great dams and kinds of dams
   i. Notable bridges.

The children select the major features of the reference they are reviewing for the class and give specific examples. While they are preparing their reports, the librarian and the teacher help them identify the major features.

For example, *Hammond's Nature Atlas of America* is very useful in an elementary school for the many science units involving nature. The main text is divided into sections as follows:

Minerals and Rocks	Fishes
Trees	Amphibians and Reptiles
Wildflowers	Insects
Birds	Climate and Nature
Animals	Landforms and Nature

Each subject is introduced by a distribution map of the United States. Following the map is a section with colored pictures on each page and simple, detailed descriptions of each picture.

Webster's Geographical Dictionary, a gazetteer, has few illustrations. It is basically an alphabetical listing of geographical places in the world, giving all pertinent information, e.g., location of a city, its founding, population, important industries, and historical features. It is a quick, convenient, single-volume reference tool.

Step 5—The children receive questions on cards to which they find the answers in these reference works.

> **HISTORICAL ATLAS OF THE UNITED STATES***
> 1. According to the map "States Effecting the Ratification of the 21st Amendment" what 3 states ratified the amendment from April-May?
> 2. According to the map "America in the Second World War: Army Camps . . ." how many naval bases were located in California?

Atlases and gazetteers contain a wealth of information that is a never-ending surprise to children who become acquainted with them.

The librarian may conclude with reviews of such books as *Kon-tiki for Young People* and *Escapes and Rescues*.

ALMANACS

Grade 5 (continued)

Step 1—The *World Almanacs* and *Information Please Almanacs* are distributed among the fifth-grade children and reviewed together. The teacher queries them on

1. How often is the almanac published?
   Once a year
2. Where is the index located in each of the two almanacs?
   World Almanac: front
   Information Please Almanac: back
3. What is a main entry?
   A main subject
4. What is the order of main entries in the index?
   Alphabetical
5. What kind of type are they in?
   Bold-face type

---

* *Historical Atlas of the United States,* Revised edition. Clifford L. Lord and Elizabeth H. Lord Copyright 1944, 1963 by Clifford L. Lord. Holt, Rinehart and Winston, Inc., Publishers.

6. What is a sub-entry in an index?
   A subject related to the main entry and indented under it
7. In what order are sub-entries arranged?
   Alphabetical
8. What do the numbers at the end of each entry stand for?
   Pages in the book
   E.g., How many pages are covered by the reference:
      250–61?   250, 61?

For interest and emphasis, the librarian may ask, "If your mother sent you to the store with a note requesting half a dozen fruits each of

```
┌─────────────────────────┐
│                         │
│   bananas, oranges      │
│                         │
└─────────────────────────┘
```

how many different kinds of fruit would you get?" . . . "Why?" . . . "Yes, only two because the comma means *and*."
   "Another time she sends you with a note requesting half a dozen fruits each of

```
┌─────────────────────────┐
│                         │
│   bananas—oranges       │
│                         │
└─────────────────────────┘
```

Name some of the fruits you would bring back." The children name

      bananas
      cherries
      grapefruit
      grapes
      lemons, etc.

but *not* peaches or strawberries, as these come *after* oranges in the alphabet; and not apples, as these come *before* bananas. But all the fruits in-between, yes. The same can be done with vegetables until the significance of the comma and the dash are made clear.

   Step 2—The children browse through the almanacs, noting the many subjects listed, to get a sense of the scope of subject matter (Figure 9–3). Emphasis is placed on the format with its numerous tables of facts and figures about persons, places, and events. Examples given may be the home runs by baseball "greats" like Babe Ruth; birth dates and real names of television stars; statistics on the world series and Olympic winners; census figures; state flowers, birds, trees;

Figure 9–3.

the monetary unit of each country; etc. The class concludes by working out a definition for an almanac, including the following points:

1. An almanac is published once a year.
2. It contains information for previous years.
3. It contains many statistical tables.
4. It contains summaries of many kinds.
5. It is a good place to locate census figures.
6. The information covers wide subject areas.
7. It is not in alphabetical order.
8. It is essential to use the index to locate information.

Step 3—After a review of the type of material found in almanacs, including the state almanacs if available, each fifth grader is given an individual card with questions to be answered from these tools. For example:

Card 1

1. **How old was the Lindbergh baby when it was kidnapped?**
   What happened to him?
2. **How long is the Amazon River?**
   Where is its outflow?

> **Card 2**
> 1. What is the nickname of Oregon?
> 2. What is the largest city in Oregon?
> 3. What is the seating capacity of the
>   Colosseum in Rome?

The children's answer sheet will look like this:

> *Card 1*   Name ....
>   Room ....
> 1. 20 months old
>   Kidnapped and killed
>   Reference: *World Almanac* 1966: 189
> 2. 3900 miles
>   Atlantic Ocean
>   Reference: *World Almanac* 1966: 290

> *Card 2*
> 1. Beaver State
> 2. Portland
>   Reference: *Information Please* 1960: 302
> 3. 40,000–50,000
>   Reference: *Information Please* 1950: 808

As the children check for answers, they quickly realize the entries in the index of different editions vary from year to year.

Children often become so interested in these reference tools that they start checking out almanacs.

INDEXES

Because of the nature of reference tools and because school libraries are apt to have only one copy of each tool discussed, the librarian will need to present each of several references by using the overhead projector and exhibiting each book as she reviews it.

Step 1—To make the lesson really meaningful the librarian gives individual instruction by means of "field work." She makes arrangements with the fifth-grade teacher for class assignments involving small groups coming to the library during free periods to look up poems, quotations, short stories, and fairy tales.

"Here is exactly the book you need!" exclaims the librarian, and six doleful faces immediately brighten. *Bartlett's Familiar Quotations* and the *Index to Fairy Tales, . . . Children's Poetry,* and . . . *Short Stories* are spread out on the library table, and the librarian is able to give small-group instruction in these indexes. This method of instructing small groups has the added advantage that the children may go immediately to the card catalog to verify whether the library owns the book, and if so, may proceed to the shelves to locate it.

The librarian will also want to introduce the *National Geographic Index* according to one of the two following methods:

A. The cumulative indexes for the bound volumes of the *National Geographics* are in two volumes: from 1899–1946 and from 1947–1963. The paper back indexes for each of the following years will, of course, eventually accumulate into additional bound volumes.

The references in the author-subject-title index give volume, pages, date, and number of illustrations for each one listed:

ABELL, GEORGE O.:
   Exploring the Farthest Reaches of Space. By
   George O. Abell. 9 illus., pp. 782–790,
   Dec., 1956

ASTRONOMY:
   Exploring the Farthest Reaches of Space. By
   George O. Abell. 9 illus., pp. 782–790,
   Dec., 1956

EXPLORING the Farthest Reaches of Space. By
   George O. Abell. 9 illus., pp. 782–790, Dec.,
   1956

In the back of this is an extensive map index, with the geographical subject in bold-face type as the main entry.

B. In schools using the individually bound pamphlets,[3] the li-

---

[3] Angwin Bindery, Angwin, California, will bind each article separately. The *Skadsheim Topical Index* is published by this company to accompany the bound articles. Subject cards for the catalog are also available from Angwin.

brarian will introduce Sections 1 and 3 of the *Skadsheim Topical Index* in some detail, and will mention Section 2.

(1) Section 1 contains the major headings:

> Natural Science
> Travel and Geography
> Europe
> Asia, Africa, and Pacific Islands
> Americas

Under each of these, different subjects are named according to the Dewey Decimal System, listing various articles on each subject, giving these in chronological order according to the dates of the *National Geographic,* e.g.,

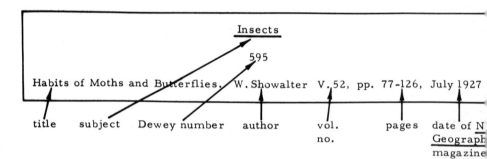

(2) Section 2 lists various topics by year of publication.

(3) Section 3 is a subject index giving the title on the pamphlet box and the articles on the subject. It is this section that is used most extensively.

Several samples on the chalkboard taken directly from Section 3 are sufficient with the explanation of the parts.

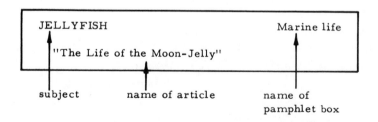

Willie and Debra, in order to illustrate how the reference is used, go to the pamphlet boxes according to the information given in the Topical Index. This is their first insight into the use of these.

As SIXTH GRADERS they make frequent use of these individually bound articles in their reference work throughout the year.

Of course these easy-to-handle, singly bound *National Geographic* articles go home as regular books, a great advantage over bound volumes.

BIOGRAPHICAL MATERIAL

Grade 5 (continued)

By transparencies and examination the children are introduced to the *Junior Book of Authors* and its supplement, *More Junior Authors*. These are books of biographical and autobiographical sketches, in some detail, of modern authors of children's books. They are arranged in alphabetical order and have the author's picture with each article. Older authors, as Alcott and Stevenson, are not included, nor are border-line authors who write books for both children and adults.

Many libraries maintain an author file, composed of clippings from magazines and book jackets. These are filed in various ways in different libraries; alphabetical arrangement in a box, folder in the vertical file, etc. The system of filing is of little importance so long as the children have easy access to the information. Often information about a current, popular author can be located here when it can be found nowhere else.

Grade 6

Biographical material, additional to that presented in grade five, can be covered for sixth graders in one lesson. The biographical section in *Webster's . . . Unabridged* was discussed with the dictionary unit. It may be pointed out again that the information given is brief: a sentence or two. It is a tool only for indentification.

Webster's Biographical Dictionary, on the other hand, is an expansion of the above-mentioned section. Just as the gazetteer section of *Webster's Unabridged* was expanded into *Webster's Geographical Dictionary,* so the biographical section was expanded into *Webster's Biographical Dictionary,* with the addition of more names and more information. For a few additional details, beyond a mere identification, the *Biographical Dictionary* is the answer.

For a biographical report of several pages, Debra would turn next to the encyclopedia. Here she will find the length of the article depends on the significance of the biographee. She would find much more information, for example, on George Washington than on Babe Ruth.

Finally, Debra may want to check the card catalog to find out whether the library has a book on the biographee.

The simplest method to demonstrate the amount of material to be found in each of these tools is to place a comparative table, as illustrated in Figure 9–4, on the chalkboard.

Here is a natural opportunity to review the author, title, and subject cards and again to discuss the perennial trouble spots:

1. What does the word *biographical* mean?
    Relating to the life of a person
2. What is the call number for individual biography?
    921 plus a letter
3. What is the difference between individual and collective biography?
    The first is the life of one person; the second is the life of two or more people
4. Are the classification numbers different?
    Yes
5. What is different about the letters under the classification numbers?
    With individual biographies, the letter refers to the biographee; with collective biographies the letter refers to the author's last name
6. Why does this differentiation occur?
    Collective biography may have the lives of several people whose last names all start with different letters

Explorers All	Lee
	Boys'
920	Life of
A	John F.
Barbara K.	Kennedy
Anthony	921
	K

Figure 9–4. Comparative table of amounts of information.

Name of Place	Webster's ... Unabridged Gazetteer Section	Webster's Geographical Dictionary, 1964	Compton's, 1966	World Book, 1964
Popocatepetl	2 lines	3½ lines	5-line Fact Summary with cross reference to 1 illustration and 1 map	Half a column; cross reference to 1 illustration
Yosemite Valley	3 lines	4 lines	Listed under Yosemite National Park. 1½ columns with 2 illustrations. Cross reference in index to 2 other volumes	Listed under Yosemite National Park. One full page (2 full columns) with 2 photographs on facing page. Six related articles

Person	Webster's ... Unabridged Biographical Section	Webster's Biographical Dictionary, 1959	Compton's, 1966	World Book, 1964	Individual biography
Clara Barton	4 words	14 lines	1 full column, 2 photographs	1 full column, 2 photographs, 1 cross reference	X
Sir Francis Drake	4 words	43 lines	1½ columns, 1 photograph, cross reference to 6 other volumes	1½ columns, 2 photographs, 2 cross references	X

Grade 6 (continued)

The librarian should bring to the children's attention other reference tools. In particular, the following can be consulted:

1. *American Book of Days:* Detailed information on holidays, festivals, notable anniversaries, arranged by days of the month from January 1 to December 31. The appendix covers the calendar, zodiac, etc. The index covers all holidays and feast days described. This tool is very popular with the children. They all want to search out the happenings on *their* birthdays.

2. *Bartlett's Familiar Quotations* gives the source of each quotation listed.

3. *Book of Popular Science:* A ten-volume encyclopedia covering the whole field of science, with an index in the last volume. Preceding the index is an excellent bibliography covering numerous subject groups:

general works on science	mathematics
the universe	matter and energy (chemistry and
the earth	physics)
life	industry
plant life	transportation
animal life	communication
man	science though the ages
health	projects and experiments

Also included are tables of scientific facts and figures, such as a list of the Nobel prize winners.

4. *Brewer's Dictionary of Phrase and Fable* is exactly what the title says. It is an extensive alphabetical list of classical references, many of them quite obscure. It also contains some slang phrases and expressions that arose from World War II. It is not used extensively at the elementary school level but can be helpful in answering questions such as "What does Project *Gemini* mean?"

5. *Commager's Encyclopedia of American History:* One volume of essential historical facts in both chronological and topical order. Dates, events, achievements, and persons of importance are given in narrative form.

6. *Famous First Facts:* The first 495 pages are an alphabetical listing, two columns per page, of the first time something happened.

E.g.:

THE FIRST	THE FIRST
ALLIGATOR FARM was established in 1892 at Anastasia Island, St. John's County, Fla., by George Reddington.	ALUMINUM STREET CAR. *See* Car.

7. *Picturesque Tale of Progress:* An excellent set of nine volumes on history from 100,000 B.C. to about 1600 A.D. It gives detailed story descriptions of such ancient civilizations as the Greeks, Incas, Mayas, and the Persians. Each volume has its own index. The last volume is an index to the entire set.

8. *Shankle's State Names, Flags, Seals, Songs, Birds, Flowers, and Other Symbols* is divided by subject, under which each state is discussed. It has a detailed index.

9. *Subject Index to Books for Primary . . .* or *For Intermediate Grades:* These two indexes name various book titles for a given subject, or list books and indicate the pages in those books containing information on the particular subject.

10. *Young People's Science Dictionary:* "designed as a companion volume to the *Young People's Science Encyclopedia.*" Besides definitions and explanations of words and ideas, the dictionary contains handy reference tables on measurement, elements, chemicals, planets, Greek alphabet, mammals, plants, scientists past and present. There are many other tables scattered throughout the text.

The ten references listed above may be passed out to Willie and Debra and their classmates. Groups of two or three children working together prepare oral reports. After each presentation the class and the librarian ask questions to clarify the description of the reference. The children take notes if they wish, as the librarian points out the basic description if this seems necessary.

When all reports and individual units of review are completed, the children have an oral drill on the references. The librarian has posted a list of these done in felt pen on tagboard so the titles may easily be read across the room. Also, each child has a dittoed copy of concise descriptions of the references with blank spaces on the left margin for the titles, e.g.:

. . . .   Annual publication covering the main events of the *previous year.*

. . . .   Information on American holidays and
feast days.

. . . .   A collection of quotations and their
sources.

Step 1—*Fun Time Drill: Identifying the References:* Each
group has a turn at selecting and reading aloud from the sheet in
front of him a description of a reference which he then identifies.
After all are accounted for, the librarian asks various questions for
which the groups name the references containing the answers. Since
the children have had drill on encyclopedias these are excluded. The
questions are stated in such a way that clues guide the child to only
one particular reference, such as

    a. When was the first balloon flight made?
    b. In ancient times where were artichokes grown?
    c. How many toes did prehistoric horses have?

The word *first* in question "a" is a give-away for *Famous First Facts.*
The word *ancient* or *prehistoric* identifies *Picturesque Tale of Progress.*

  Sometimes the children search out their own questions when they
work with these tools and such questions often form the basis for
general practice and review.

Step 2—*Digging In:* Each child receives an individual card
containing two to four questions:

---

1. The *Bloodhound* in 1960 was a space missile of what
   country?
   Give its length in feet and its range in miles.
2. In 1962 the *Thor-Agena B* was flown how many
   times?

---

1. When was the first open air post office established?
2. Which part of the United States has the most manufacturing areas?
3. What was a woolly rhinoceros in ancient times?
4. What is the elevation of Salt Lake City?

> 1. **What cities are directly north and south of Portland, Oregon?**
> 2. **What is the capital of Iceland?**
> 3. **Name four continents that border the Atlantic Ocean.**
> 4. **What is the largest man-made lake in the western United States?**

The children record the questions, give brief answers and the source of each answer, excluding encyclopedias. Some children may cover three or four cards while others do only one, each working at his own speed and capability. The reference list on tagboard is in view at all times and the children have the dittoed lists which were filled out earlier.

One variation is to have several "digging in" sessions after each four or five tools are presented and discussed. If time allows for this drill, students will profit by studying and using five or six tools at a time rather than en masse.

Step 3—Time Out! After several sessions spent on "referencing" for the answers to questions, the class may become weary of this drill. Time out! The pace is changed to revive enthusiasm. The librarian returns the papers at the next round for a game. From their papers, Table 1 reads a question to Table 2. Table 2 states the correct source or reference and receives a colored tab. Should Table 2 give the incorrect answer, Table 1 receives the tab for the correct one. Then Table 2 asks Table 3 a question, etc. Near the end of the game, each table tallies its tabs to decide the winner. In a tie, the tables involved answer questions posed by the losing tables.

Step 4—Reference Bingo:[4] At last comes the final session: a reference bingo game (Figure 9–5). Each one receives a dittoed "bingo" sheet on which he fills each square with a different reference title from those listed on an accompanying sheet. The list contains more titles than the number of squares. Small colored squares of construction paper are placed on each table—the use of corn is obviously out of the question! When all have filled in the sheet with the titles

---

4 Game developed by Lora Palovic.

Figure 9–5.

in whatever order or arrangement each wishes, the librarian states the rules of the game:

1. All titles need to be spelled correctly.
2. No colored squares are accepted with writing on them.
3. The librarian calls off a key description.[5] Each one decides for himself which reference it is and places a square on that title if he has marked it on his sheet. The librarian may have a stack of cards, one for each title, with or without the description. As she calls each description, she lays the card on the table as a check against the answers a winner calls back.

4. Reference bingo occurs when the player has covered
     a. The four corners,
     b. A diagonal,
     c. A straight across, or
     d. A straight down.
5. The player then calls REFERENCE BINGO.
6. When several players call REFERENCE BINGO at the same time, they each get a turn at calling back the answers, with the teacher or librarian checking his sheet.
7. Once someone starts giving the answers, no one else may bingo on that round if he did not notify the librarian before the first answer or title is called.
8. If errors occur, explanations are given on why the answer is incorrect and what the incorrect answer refers to, and the game continues. As a result, if no one scores, the class continues for a single bingo.

---

5 See the ten descriptions on pages 142–143 of this chapter.

9. When a player bingos, the game continues for a double bingo, *adding* to the answers already given for single bingo; then a triple (perhaps even a quad or quint), and finally blackout.

10. If no blackout occurs before the last title is to be called, the librarian recalls two titles given earlier in the game; otherwise, the whole class would score, which creates a difficult situation when "prizes" are given. Sometimes in just a natural line-up, however, only one person blacks out on the next to the last title in the complete list given.

REFERENCE BINGO

For advanced groups the game may be more challenging by having the winner describe each title he calls back. Also, when too many have REFERENCE BINGO, the number of winners may be narrowed by the same procedure.

When new books are being processed for circulation, each winner may jot on a slip of paper his name and the title of one of these books, tagging it to indicate he will be the *first* to read it when it is ready. This often puts the pressure on the librarian as she promises to have the tagged books ready at the next library visit. The librarian needs to explain clearly that the "prize" is not for keeps!

REFERENCE TOOLS FOR REFERENCE BINGO

American Book of Days
Bartlett's Familiar Quotations
Book of Popular Science
Britannica Book of the Year
Britannica Junior Encyclopaedia
Card Catalog
Compton's Pictured Encyclopedia
Dewey Decimal Classification
Encyclopedia of American History
Famous First Facts
Global Atlas
Historical Atlas of the United States
Index to Fairy Tales
Index to Poetry
Information Please Almanac
Junior Book of Authors
Lincoln Library of Essential Information
National Geographic Index
Picturesque Tale of Progress
Short Story Index
Subject Index to Books . . .
Unabridged dictionary
Vertical file
Webster's Biographical Dictionary
Webster's Geographical Dictionary
World Almanac
World Atlas
World Book Encyclopedia

Chapter 10—

Joyful Moments in the Library—

The Story Hour and

Literature Program

Wide-open eyes, expectant silence, a crackling fire—bright faces all upturned to the storyteller: nothing can surpass the satisfaction that comes from seeing each child hanging eagerly on every word of the story (Figure 10–1). The teacher comments: "The children so look forward to their story time that I don't dare forget it!"

A librarian needs to be well-prepared to reward such anticipation if she expects to maintain interest and enthusiasm. The selections,

Figure 10–1.

especially for the beginning librarian, need to be chosen with great care. Of two choice stories, one may be "Away-She-Go," taken from a book entitled *Injun Babies*. This is the story of the little Indian girl (the word "injun" is never used by the authors!) who is always running away from her tepee and one day falls into a bears' hole. The children love the contrasting voices of Away-She-Go, Father Bear, and "Daddy," and they especially enjoy "finger climbing" to the top of the hole with the bears and with Away-She-Go.

> "Finger climbing": the librarian leads the children in tapping their shoulders for the climbing. They tap the shoulders for Mama Bear's climbing. They then tap (in the air) a few inches higher for Brother Bear and likewise higher for Sister Bear. Finally they stretch as high as their hands will reach to "tap" Sister Bear's shoulders where Baby Bear climbs.

Another choice story is *The Gunniwolf* in which the children pick flowers and sing with the little girl who forgets her mother's warning. Through finger and hand actions they chase the little girl with the "hunkercha" racing of the gunniwolf and they escape with her, each child wriggling the index and middle fingers, as she "pitty-pats" home.

> (1) To "pitty-pat," each child wriggles the index and middle fingers on each hand, moving the hands from left to right to indicate running.
> (2) To "hunkercha," each child waves the hands straight up and down as far as the elbow bends. This is done rapidly in time with sound of "hunkercha."

Other stories with action are *Lambikin, Travels of a Fox,* and *The Cat and the Parrot*. The children friskily sing the reply that Lambikin gives to the jackal and other creatures who meet and want to feast on the dainty morsel. They also count the days Lambikin stays in Granny's corn bin and they trundle along home with him until the jackal surprisingly puts an end to his foolhardiness.

In the *Travels of a Fox,* the children throw the bag over their shoulders and travel along with the fox. They enter into the spirit of the story by repeating the same remarks to each housewife and with satisfaction hear the fate of the fox.

They "trip trap" over the bridge with the *Three Billy Goats Gruff* and "butt their horns" into the troll and throw the pieces into the river.

How they love to mimic the parrot in *The Cat and the Parrot*—and such laughter and surprised faces as the parade of creatures disappears down the cat's gullet!

Although many children may be accustomed to audio-visual aids in story-telling, such as pop-up books, flannelboard stories, puppets, etc., a librarian need not resort to these to hold her audience. A good piece of literature well told will hold the attention of kindergartners and older children. Even their teachers enjoy the library story hour. No gimmicks are needed for *The Gingerbread Man, Scrapefoot, The Three Billy Goats Gruff.*

For variety, the story hour may be punctuated with such action packed stories as a jungle adventure (make up your own hand and foot movements and sounds), or the action song *Little Cabin in the Woods.* Kindergartners and first graders delight in giving the finger and hand movements through each singing. On the last round they give the actions for the entire song in silence.

A dramatic variation is having an artist illustrate a story as the librarian tells it. It is effective in a darkened room with a spotlight on the artist. It has been done beautifully in pastel chalk with *Lambikin; The Tiger, Brahman, and the Jackal;* and *The Gunniwolf.*

Or, the children may do the illustrating. The story needs to be told first for familiarity. At the second telling the children participate with art work. Appropriate background music adds to the creative mood and enhances the illustrations. This actually is better done in the classroom where interruptions are less apt to occur. (See Figure 10–2.)

Lucky is the school that has a large library with a fireplace and radiant heating! The children are free to sit in whatever manner they wish on the floor to try their artistic talents.

Again the children may scatter over the floor for some paper-folding fun. Each one follows directions connected with the demonstration of making a box from a piece of paper. The librarian illustrates and explains, and the teacher helps the children. Books on origami and Chinese paper folding become sellouts the rest of the year.

And then the class returns to just listening wide-eyed to the magic of the story—no props, just a well-learned and well-told story (Figure 10–3). The voice and the eyes control the entire picture. A pleasant, appealing atmosphere adds another dimension. Thus, the

Drawing by Tom Santillan, San Miguel School, Sunnyvale, California.

Figure 10–2.

Figure 10–3.

young child has an indelible picture of a library hour that may greatly affect his attitude toward the library the rest of his life.

If he doesn't get this as a kindergartner, it isn't too late. Lasting library impressions can happen in any grade. One upper grade boy made it a point to have a pass to the library during at least one primary story hour each week. Though he came presumably for reference, the librarian knew he chose this time to enjoy the story, for he sat without a reference book the whole time. He often came in weekly, when the story was a continued one, such as *Budulinek,* which can easily be divided where Budulinek disappears from home.

The stories may become a little longer from one grade to the next. The third through sixth grades thrill to *Clever Manka.* It's fun to tease by stopping with the riddle to keep them guessing at the solution till the following week. E.g., how will Manka go to the burgomaster's "neither by day nor by night, neither walking nor riding, neither dressed nor undressed?" Or, the children might give their answers to what is the swiftest thing in the world, the sweetest, the richest, before they hear Manka's answer.

The Chippewa Indian tale, *Shingebiss,* is a beautiful story. The sturdy little brown duck who loved his fellow creatures even though they tried to destroy him appeals to all ages. The Indian folk song he sings is a haunting melody that long remains after the story is told. *From Tiger to Anansi* also is a real spellbinder.

No age is immune to a story well-told; and a story of genuine literary quality, suspense, intrigue, and reality enthralls both young and old. The librarian who masters episodes from the *Iliad* and the *Odyssey* can entrance teenagers. Even the rowdy and undisciplined ones may succumb, as did one particular senior class, to the librarian's dramatic presentation of Patrick Henry's "Give me liberty or give me death."

The storyteller may wish to consult the following:

1. Jeanne B. Hardendorff, rev. and ed. by, *Stories to Tell,* A list of stories with annotations (Baltimore, Md.: Enoch Pratt Free Library, 1965) . 83 pages.
2. Ellin Greene, comp., *Stories,* A list of stories to tell and to read aloud (New York: N.Y. Public Library, 1965) . 78 pages.
3. Ruth Sawyer, *The Way of the Storyteller.* Rev. ed. (New York: Viking, 1962) .
4. Frances Clarke Sayers, *Summoned by Books* (New York: Viking, 1965) . "The Telling of Tales" pages 95–106.

5. Marie Shedlock, *The Art of the Story-Teller* (New York: Dover Publications, 1951).

6. Gudrun Thorne-Thomsen, *Story-telling and Stories I Tell* (New York: Viking, 1956).

As children hear story after story, and along the way become aware of such characters as Paul Bunyan or Stormalong, Thor or Perseus, Peter Rabbit or Christopher Robin, the librarian may vary the program by having the children create a group story, or having each one do a creative piece. The following poem was the result of a creative group activity directed by the librarian during a story time; Willie suggested the ideas be incorporated into a poetic form:

Swinging on a Cobweb[1]

If I could swing on a cobweb in the sky,
I could take a ride on a bird flying by.

If I got hungry I could eat
A marshmallow cloud for a treat.

If I got thirsty after I play
I could take a drink from the Milky Way.

If I could visit a fairy living on the stars
She might even take me to visit Mars.

And if my cobweb should break
I might even land on Cloud 88.

If we jump up and down like a trampoline
We might even catch the cobweb dream.

The value of reading aloud as well as telling stories cannot be too strongly stressed. Sometimes reading directed toward one group may catch other fish in the net.

A fourth grade was listening raptly to the story of Perseus and the Gorgon's Head from Sellew's *Adventures with the Gods* when two rather sophisticated sixth grade boys of the "guns, racing cars, army" set dropped into the library. They browsed along the shelves and as the story went on their interest in choosing a book obviously waned. In the course of the librarian's story where the picture of the three witches handing around their one eye was passed from table to table, the boys too took a quick look.

As the librarian closed the book, one of the boys immediately asked if he could have it. The other, obviously disgruntled that he

---

[1] Mrs. Thelma Cox's second grade, Jarvis E. Bishop Elementary School, Sunnyvale, California, February, 1965.

hadn't got there first, muttered, "What's the number on that book?" He located another 291 with the same story and the two went off happily to sample, probably for the first time in their lives, some of the Greek myths.

THE LITERATURE PROGRAM

From the very beginning, the library stresses books of lasting value. The book collection is built up first according to recognized basic lists. These books meet the needs of children in their joys and search for knowledge. Other books are added for their literary values and for the needs of the curriculum and interest of the children. Unless they accidentally stumble on them, children have no means of knowing the interesting books if these are not brought to their attention. Once the Caldecott and Newbery Award books are introduced, many become steady choices. The more the librarian reads, the better prepared she is to influence the children in their reading; for, of course, to sell one's wares, one must be familiar with them. The broader the librarian's knowledge of a book collection, the more effectively she meets the needs of each child and guides him into books that relate to his needs and his pleasures.

When the kindergartners visit the library for story time, they hear exciting stories. Often these are classics which form a continuous thread from kindergarten on. In reviewing books for the first graders who are just beginning to check them out, the librarian displays and reviews these favorite stories which have stood the test of time. In grades two and three she continues reviews. Booklists, with reading levels indicated, may be passed out at appropriate times during the year.

In the intermediate grades, longer reviews are given and excerpts from the books are read. The librarian introduces an informal discussion of "What is literature?" by quoting from Paul Hazard's *Books, Children and Men* (chap. 1):

> Liberators will come, from Grimm to Andersen; and there will be others later on, but before them, around them, how many pedants and fools there were! How many exploiters trying to make a profit from worthless merchandise! What a cemetery!
> You may say: It is all very well to look disgusted. What does please you, anyway, and just what are you asking for? Stories, nothing but stories? Do you grow angry as soon as knowledge or morals

is mentioned? And for a book to satisfy you, must it contain absolutely nothing? First of all, I reply, there are good books of every kind; and when one of them is good, even though it does not contain what I ask for, let it be welcomed gratefully. . . .

By much questioning the librarian draws from the children answers revolving around

Imagination	Reality	Plot
Illustrations	Humor	Theme
Character growth	Originality	Style

The librarian may read an excerpt from the originals of *Tom Sawyer, Cinderella,* or *Robinson Crusoe* and the same section in an adapted version. By comparing the two the children realize that a controlled and simplified vocabulary, which necessitates changing the wording of the original, destroys much of the color, leaving only the bare plot.

An accelerated group is able to deal with much detail and study. One such class read Fea's *Adventure in the Sierras* and discussed at length whether this book could qualify as a classic. The librarian, as moderator, offered no opinion and only occasionally ventured a question. The group unanimously agreed that, although it was a good story, it had too many shortcomings to be excellent literature.

Finally each child may produce a creative piece which can bring much humor and pleasure to the group. The children act as critics, pointing out what the would-be author has done well and how he may improve on the weak points. They become aware that they have much potential, for often a group will readily acknowledge some of their creativeness as truly classic writing. Publication of their creations in the school's creative writing journal is genuine incentive to better writing and better communication.

The librarian is, of course, constantly aware that the reading level in each grade covers a wide span. A poor reader or a disadvantaged child, e.g., in the sixth grade could be hopelessly lost to reading if he heard only about *A Wrinkle in Time, The Jungle Book, Ginger Pye.* He may need to hear about *Curious George, Joji and the Fog,* or *Huge Harold.* When this is his reading level, the alert librarian will understandingly and gladly see him take these books home. It is a joy to hear the slower sixth grader laugh at picture books, for from these he may gradually be led to the Eddie books, the Piggle-Wiggle books, *Henry Huggins, Ben and Me,* and *Homer Price.*

Films on the classics, enjoyed by all children, may stimulate a reluctant reader into attempting something more difficult than he otherwise might have chosen. Add to the Weston Woods filmstrips that reproduce such books as *Millions of Cats,* these outstanding films:

> . . . *And Now Miguel*
> *The Doughnuts*
> *Heidi*
> *Johnny Appleseed*
> *The Steadfast Tin Soldier*
> *The Story of a Book* (*Pagoo*)
> *Treasure Island*
> *The Ugly Duckling*

The enthusiastic librarian can greatly influence a child in his reading through her knowledge of books, her wise selection of stories for telling, her awareness of the many ways and possibilities in which a child may actively participate in story-telling, and her selection of titles for book reviews. Her enthusiasm and guidance may be responsible for establishing in the child the lifetime library habit. It may inspire him into serious creative writing and eventually to authorship.

Chapter 11—

Cabbages and Kings—

Taking Care of

"Miscellany"

Every library school finds itself with a collection of flotsam and jetsam that does not fit neatly into any course. The tendency is to lump this miscellanea together and offer "Social Functions of the Library" or "The Library and Society" or another course with an equally ambiguous and all-inclusive title.

Just so, the school librarian finds herself with odds and ends that need to be fitted into the skills curriculum. E.g., reading enrichment is a theme that runs through the entire school term, year after year. The presentation of periodicals is flexible; it may be presented from fourth to sixth grades alone or correlated with some other unit. Such material has all been brought into this chapter.

ENRICHMENT READING

What is enrichment reading? It may consist of many elements, have many facets, embrace several aspects of reading beyond the basic classroom program. It has different meanings for different people:

1. Gaining an understanding and appreciation of the culture of various periods
2. Gaining an insight and understanding of oneself

3. Resolving personal problems through reading about others' experiences
4. Learning worthwhile ways of using leisure time

Of course, teacher and librarian work together on any enrichment program.

Any such program undertaken by the librarian necessitates an interested principal, a cooperative teacher, and a librarian with a flexible schedule. The group in a reading enrichment program may be gifted children, or very slow readers who need a small-group experience where their slowness will not contrast with the pace of more intelligent children. Or it may involve average children who need extra attention to spark their interest. Experience indicates that eight children make a good group and that with more than twelve the group loses potency.

One group may operate successfully as follows: when the group meets in the library, each child silently reads a chapter from the same title the first half of the period. The second half may be open to conversation about the material read. Many children, to whom writing is extremely distasteful, enjoy the give-and-take of an informal discussion. The librarian becomes a listener, only occasionally prodding a child who is reluctant to speak or toning down more vocal members of the group.

Anything in the nature of a "book report" is to be discouraged as are homework assignments, particularly for a slow or reluctant reading group, for this is an activity to spur and enrich the child's reading. Making it an assignment defeats the purpose. The child may then in all probability neglect the assignment and come with dragging feet to the reading group, disinterested and unprepared to participate.

The discussion may wander far afield from the chapters read, but there is no harm in this and there is often some value. One group, reading Gipson's *Old Yeller*, fell into a discussion of home remedies for various illnesses, and the librarian was electrified to discover how many children in the group, in this age of clinics and health insurance, are still treated to hot whiskey toddies to cure a cold! The same group was fascinated with colloquialisms, an entirely new word to them, and spent much time selecting and analyzing these from each chapter of *Old Yeller*.

Figure 11–1.

If the children wish a culminating activity, they may make drawings or clay models of their favorite scenes or characters (Figure 11–1). These may be held for exhibit in the library during open house week. When one book is finished, the demands to "do another book" destroy any doubts the librarian has as to the success of this project.

An area rich in possibilities for enrichment reading is that of the social studies. Almost every unit of social studies in the elementary grades has a bibliography of good fiction books to accompany it. What better way is there for a child to get the "feel" of a period of history than to read *Wind in the Chimney, Elin's Amerika, The Witch of Blackbird Pond,* or *Across Five Aprils?*

Biographies of scientists or inventors may be read in conjunction with science units. For example, the following:

Benjamin Franklin by Irmengarde Eberle
Copernicus by Henry Thomas
The Curies and Radium by Elizabeth Rubin
Galileo and the Magic Numbers by Sidney Rosen
Louis Pasteur by Mary Burton
Mr. Bell Invents the Telephone by Katherine Shippen
Thomas Alva Edison by G. Clark

Biographies of authors add greatly to the reading of such books as *Treasure Island* and *Little Women*. For example:

Invincible Louisa by Cornelia Meigs
The Treasure Hunter by Isabel Proudfit
Why They Wrote by Rhoda Hoff

Along with these literary pieces, the story of the Caldecott and Newbery awards is given. How did they originate? Who receives them? Such a background naturally leads into the meaning of the word "classic." A display of Caldecott and Newbery winners offers an opportunity to point out modern illustrating and bookmaking at their best.
Underline each title once.

PUZZLE STORY ON THE CALDECOTT WINNERS

There was always room for one more in the little house where Abraham Lincoln once lived. Mei Lei listened there to the song of the swallows as they flew over the egg tree. Nearby where the tree is nice was the biggest bear who had just come to Madeline's rescue!

Over on the other side of the little island the finders keepers were adding to the ruckus caused by Chanticleer and the fox.

It was a time of wonder. Even frog went a' courtin' Cinderella while Sam, Bangs, and Moonshine waited many moons for the big snow.

Finally it was a snowy day: white snow bright snow covered the little island. The animals of the Bible gathered where the wild things are. They all waited with Baboushka during the nine days to Christmas. They were strong and good as they said many a prayer for a child.

On this island anyone who asked, "May I bring a friend?" could do so even if he was once a mouse. And all worked hard to make way for ducklings who wanted to make their home too on the little island.

PUZZLE STORY ON THE NEWBERY WINNERS[1]

Underline each title once.

Strawberry girl hung her roller skates on the door in the wall and went to play on rabbit hill with Ginger Pye at her heels. She had with her her doll Hitty who had been one of the miracles on Maple Hill. Hitty had lived in the early days of the matchlock gun and Johnny Tremain and she had survived rifles for Watie!

Before the time when her cat that went to heaven lived, strawberry girl used to talk to her: "It's like this, cat: I'd like to sail away on twenty-one balloons and meet Mrs. Whosits in that wrinkle in time. That's a long time since the bronze bow.

"And couldn't we have fun if we could carry on (with) Mr. Bowditch as we sailed on the dark frigate to the island of blue dolphins. There would be no witch of blackbird pond there! We might even meet some of the animals that were seen on the voyages of Dr. Dolittle.

"Then we could sail on to South America and find out the secret of the Andes. I wonder if Waterless Mountain has anything to do with it.

"Well, from there we'd go on to China to talk with young Fu of the upper Yangtze. We might be lucky enough to get acquainted with Shen of the sea.

"But—oh—run, Ginger Pye, run! That's no white stag yonder. It's the shadow of a bull coming toward us! Oh, for Smoky or the king of the wind to help us out!

"Thank goodness, we're safe. I wouldn't call it courage to be foolish enough to face him: for, I'm not an invincible Louisa or an Onion John!"

Then strawberry girl went homeward, speaking on the way to Amos Fortune, free man. He had just finished reading I Juan de Pareja and was starting on Dobry. So strawberry girl hurried home to listen to her grandfather's tales from silver lands.

In the middle of these she turned on the television to watch Daniel Boone who had stopped to listen to the trumpeter of Krakow. He saw Gay Neck flying overhead, following Caddie Woodlawn. Caddie was talking to Adam of the road who was returning from putting the wheel on the school.

. . . And now Miguel came up the road slowly. That was another milestone indeed in the story of mankind. . . . . Then strawberry girl fell asleep with Miss Hickory, a fitting end to her thimble summer.

The possibilities for the form and arrangement of enrichment

---

1 Both stories by L. Palovic.

units are limited only by the teacher's or the librarian's imagination. Through these enrichment activities, the children view broad new horizons opening before them throughout the year.

SUPPLEMENTARY READING MATERIAL

The variety of books in most libraries ranges from books of quality to supplementary readers. Though much debate occurs on including supplementary readers, this type of material does have a place in the school library.

In the school short of library time and personnel, and with a large enrollment, the first and second graders often do not have frequent access to the library. To insure an ample supply of supplementary reading material for these children, each fall soon after school opens the brightly painted "tote" boxes go down the corridor to the second grade rooms. These "tote" box books, in addition to the classroom collection, are used for leisure reading in the classroom; they also go home with the children. "Tote" boxes contain some hard-backed texts and many of the beginning-to-read books such as those in the Follett Beginning-to-Read Series, the Harper, Rowe I-Can-Read Series, and the Beckley-Cardy. As these children's reading ability increases, titles by such authors as Beim, Ardizzone, and Austin are added. At the beginning of the second semester, the first grades also receive "tote" boxes.

While the books provided in the "tote" boxes are far from great works of literature, the program is important in providing many books for first and second graders at their reading levels and interests; remedial reading teachers also find such collections very helpful. Furthermore, these books are available when they are wanted. The program is important in its role of accustoming a child to reading for enrichment, on his own, when he has a little leisure, outside the classroom reading circle. Once this pattern is set, the child often carries it on to the upper grades where books of lasting value replace the "easy" books of the primary grades.

CREATIVE WRITING

Creative writing is another area in which the library may become part of the core curriculum. This enriches the work done in the classroom through discussions of books of enduring value as described in the literature program in Chapter 10.

The librarian may feature special sessions on creative writing with individual classes, making the creative writing a joint class activity on such subjects as

"The tulip that wouldn't blossom"
"The bookworm that almost got squashed"
"Swinging on a cobweb"

These are often finished and written in the classroom individually or as a single unit and published in the school literary magazine.

The librarian may work with a gifted group, going into detail on various phases of colorful literary expression and originality. The group takes time to evaluate and point out ways to improve their attempts. These also are included in the school publication.

The librarian may act as a member of the school committee which reviews and evaluates the many entries from all classes and directs their publication. She also, like the classroom teacher, gives the children guidance in communicating their ideas and writing down their stories with clarity and color. Every child enjoys seeing his name in print as the publications appear through the school year.

The librarian further fosters interest by pointing out that a magazine such as *Hornbook* does accept and pay for children's creative writing. Any child interested in submitting a piece of writing receives any needed help.

Looking at mounted pictures or listening to a record may stimulate productive creative writing periods, with the children writing or telling a story that these media may conjure up. One kindergarten group had a long-remembered experience listening to several color poems from *Hailstones and Halibut Bones* and then, as a class, producing its own poems designed around other colors.

Through these activities in creative writing children become aware of expressing themselves with clarity and vividness. They unconsciously begin to evaluate the books they read through their own experiences in writing. What more can a librarian want?!

PERIODICALS

Stimulating ch   n to submitting their creative writing for publication gives meaning to lessons on magazines. Without planned lessons, many children though they use and enjoy magazines know very little about the makeup of these library tools. Almost any free time in the library will see Willie working the puzzles in *Jack and Jill.* Fifth graders may be engrossed in a diagram in *Model Airplane News,* while fourth graders enjoy the stories in the *Golden Magazine.* Sixth grade boys clamor for the most recent copy of *Road and Track,* and all ages profitably browse through the *National Geographic.*

Yet ask the children to name the articles in magazines and they may answer "Letters to the Editor" or "Travel Directory." Ask them how to subscribe to a magazine and one hand may go up. Many children do not know how to fill in and mail an advertisement form. Some children, eyes caught by the general similarity of each month's issue of a magazine, are amazed to learn that each copy contains material different from any other.

A periodical unit need not be long. The essential information, with a short drill, may be given to a class in two sessions. It is appropriate at any grade level from fourth on. Pertinent points, however, should be covered before formal instruction in bibliography is given in the sixth grade.

When the class arrives in the library each child finds a magazine at his place. A wide assortment of titles helps to emphasize clearly the various points during the discussion.

Each child is asked to look through his magazine carefully to note how many things here are different from a book. When the children have had time to do this, the points mentioned are written in two columns on the chalkboard:

Book	*Magazine*
Usually one story	Many stories and/or articles
Usually hard cover	Paper cover
No advertisements	Advertisements
Few pictures	Many pictures
Pictures, often drawings	Pictures, usually photographs
Identification on spine	Often spine too narrow for identification
Greater cost	Single copies inexpensive
No subscription	Subscription for several months
	Publication at spaced intervals
Usually one author	Many authors

Not all these points will come to light without considerable probing by the librarian, and she may often have to raise several of the points herself.

The class then discusses various types of magazines, e.g., fun, hobbies, sports, travel, current events. Each student has a chance to give the name of his magazine and to state the kind of magazine he thinks it is. A spread of six or eight copies of the same magazine serves to show the children the difference between the title of the magazine and the names of any lead stories or articles which also appear on the cover. The librarian points out that not only does the magazine itself have a name, but each story and article has its own name and frequently its own author. Does the class clearly understand the meaning of the word "article"? This may need to be clarified even for sixth graders.

Willie and Debra are asked to take their magazines to the classroom and, with the teacher's help, find a story or article which bears out the kind of magazine each says he has. They are asked to write down this brief information:

1. Title of magazine
2. Type of magazine
3. Title of story or article
4. Short summary of story or article

They hand these to the librarian at their next library visit.

This lesson covers the make-up of a magazine. Here may be discussed sections which appear regularly and are not articles: advertisements, the table of contents, the editorial section. The space listing the editor may be located and the children learn that sometimes the material in a magazine is written by paid authors, sometimes by the editorial staff of the magazine, sometimes by both.

The children now search for the month, year, and volume number of the magazine, the place of publication, the subscription cost, and the cost for a single copy. These are usually in fine print near the table of contents and are often difficult for the children to locate. The librarian needs to ascertain that each child has actually located such information in his magazine.

To make the lessons have real meaning, children may write for information on articles of interest or recommend articles on certain subjects for future issues of the magazine. They may write a short letter subscribing to the magazine. Included are

1. Name of magazine

2. Address of magazine
3. The starting month and year
4. Volume number
5. Cost per year

They are encouraged to send in original material. Such experiences can be correlated with their creative writing and thence become meaningful in the literature enrichment program.

ASSEMBLIES

Throughout various units the classics again and again appear. Book Week is a special time to emphasize well-known books such as *Tom Sawyer* and the Caldecott and Newbery winners through assembly programs. Children gladly participate in dramatizing excerpts or character skits; presenting book plays like *Off the Shelf;* puppetry for which a class can write the play, producing their own puppets, props, and stage.

The Library and Drama clubs may collaborate in a program for National Library Week. The following describes one such joint effort, with an international theme. Interwoven with the Drama Club play *Alice in Bookland* were the variety numbers by the library assistants. (See Figure 11–2.)

Brahm's Lullaby was sung by a fifth grade tenor to whom the librarian had taught the German words. . . . The Philippine Duck Dance was taught to the library assistants by the Philippine teacher on the staff and the librarian . . . The surprise conclusion of the two men from Mars with their humor and rhythm set to music emphasized the international interest in space. . . . Printed programs which included a list of book titles relating to the performance were passed out to each child, including the guests who were library assistants from another school.

The library from time to time may emphasize the culture of a particular country. During the unit on Mexico in grade six, the librarian shows her films with a running commentary on the country. She displays many artifacts and gives firsthand information on the culture of the country which she has visited. The children listen wide-eyed as she shows the needle and thread made from maguey and as she talks about the Mexican pottery and handwoven materials on display.

NATIONAL LIBRARY WEEK

April 12 - 17

DRAMA CLUB and the LIBRARY CLUB

Present

ALICE in BOOKLAND

Bishop Elementary School   Sunnyvale

April 16: 1 p. m.   April 17: 9 a. m.

ALICE IN BOOKLAND......... Drama Club

In order of appearance

Alice
Duchess
White Rabbit
Peter Pan
Captain Hook
Page
Cowardly Lion
King
Queen
Mad Hatter
March Hare
Heidi
Miss Brown
Jane
Robin Hood

Courtiers:

Stage and costume crew:

Variety Numbers........ LIBRARY CLUB

In order of appearance

Saxophone duet
Piano duet
Pattie'bar, Irish dance
Guitar solo
Clarinet solo
Brahm's Lullaby in German
Ballet duet
Chalk talk
Chipmunk song duet

Philippine duck dance:

Men from Mars in "authentic costume"
     and dance routine

Today's program tells you about books
that are keys to joy and happiness in
your free time. Some examples with their
call numbers are

Alice in Wonderland..............	Fic C
American Folk Songs for	
Children....................	784 S
Catseye.........................	Fic L
Chalk Talk Manual............	741.23 T
Cottage at Bantry Bay............	Fic V
Dance Dance Dance...............	394 F
Dancing Star....................	921 P
First Steps in Ballet...........	792.8 M
Making an Orchestra.............	785 C
Music Across the Country........	780 M
Story of Ping	E F
Timothy's Tunes	780 M
Treasury of Plays for	
Children...................	822.08 M
Wrinkle in Time	Fic L

Figure 11-2.

The librarian who has a generous knowledge of the culture from which she stems may present priceless moments to foster international understanding. Dressed in native Yugoslavian costume, she becomes a colorful mistress of ceremonies along with the similarly dressed child at her side. She introduces the guests, immigrants from Yugoslavia, many of whom are known to some of the children. She and her little helper also introduce the native dance, the KOLO, which the children, dressed in bright costumes, have learned in physical education. Another group sings folk songs in Slavic, taught to them by the librarian. The librarian also narrates a typical folk tale of the country. At the end of the program the audience is invited to the library where many artifacts, books, and musical instruments are displayed depicting the country and its people.

Such a program often stems from a particular interest of a faculty member who may inspire the entire staff into a most stimulating crash program.

Another example is related here because it may seem most unusual for a program on Japanese customs to stem from an administrator whose great interest is conservation. But this one involved the entire school during their Japan week. Present at the planting of the cherry tree were the Japanese consulate, Japanese parents, and the priest to bless the tree. The cafeteria luncheon menu was printed in both Japanese and English. Haiku and origami art work decorated the place mats for the dignitaries. These decorations of course came through the library where each class on its regular scheduled time attended a Japanese program. They listened to Japanese music. They learned about the costume of the Japanese woman, with the librarian explaining each part of the costume which she modeled. They listened to descriptions of Japanese customs as they viewed the exhibit in the library. Before leaving, they heard the librarian relate such Japanese folk tales as *Three Strong Women* or *The Dancing Kettle*.

Triggered and directed by an enthusiastic administrator, it was a perfect example of how the whole school including the library correlated their efforts on classroom teaching and learning.

Other assemblies which foster interest in books may feature guitar-playing Sam Hinton or real, live authors. Many children have never seen an author and they often are pleasingly shocked to discover that authors are live people. An author like Ralph Moody or illustrators like Don Freeman and Leo Politi cast a spell of enchantment over their audiences. The enchantment spills over and results in an extensive run on authors' and illustrators' books.

Such programs indicate the broad furrow that the library cuts across the general school program. Many children unconsciously accept the library as part of their school community and their daily life. Not until many years later will they realize that a librarian may play a great part in their joys of learning and influence them in their ways of living.

LIBRARY ASSISTANTS' PROGRAM

One of the programs that has lasting influence on children is the library assistants' program.[2] The intimate relationship existing among children, books, and the librarian has a strong influence on the children who participate in the program. (See Figures 11–3 and 11–4.)

---

2 For another successful type of library assistants' program see Barbara Benezra and Elizabeth B. Goodman, "Helpers or Headaches," *School Libraries,* 13, No. 3 (March, 1964).

Figure 11–3.

Figure 11-4.

"Teacher, when do I get to work at the checkout counter?" . . .
"Can't I stamp the books?" . . . "Why can't we put the cards in the
books?" When the librarian is deluged with such eager questions,
she simply must take heed and do something to satisfy the desires
and needs of these children. Here is the opportunity to instruct them
in the elementary routines of librarianship and prepare the way for
prospective librarians. In the majority of schools—one needs to face
it—the librarian could scarcely get along without the help of these
enthusiasts.

It is constantly amazing to discover the many facets in which children on the elementary level are capable, both in learning and in
doing. Their brightness, their curiosity, their enthusiasm are overwhelming. Feeding these and testing them in various fields of their
interests and needs are never-ending challenges to every teacher and
librarian. (See Figure 11-5.)

Some form of a library assistants' program is an obvious means of
channeling this curiosity, enthusiasm, and desire to help. Such a pro-

gram is in no sense of the word an exploitation of elementary school children. Rather, it is excellent training for developing responsibility. They learn to be punctual, to work independently, to be reliable, to listen and follow instructions, to organize and to develop good work habits. All this is good preparation and training for their future work. In addition, as they receive recognition at the end of the year, they have the personal satisfaction of knowing they have successfully completed a job.

When she calls for voluntary library assistants, the librarian may be overwhelmed by the number that descend upon her and wonder how she will ever handle them. But by working out some standards and regulations for membership in a library assistants' program, she finds that many children voluntarily drop out, leaving a core of good workers.

For the program to be worthwhile, the librarian knows the children need to be active in it. She therefore presents a list of the basic regulations at the first meeting. Those who wish to continue take home notices for the parents' approval of their participation in the program.

Figure 11-5.

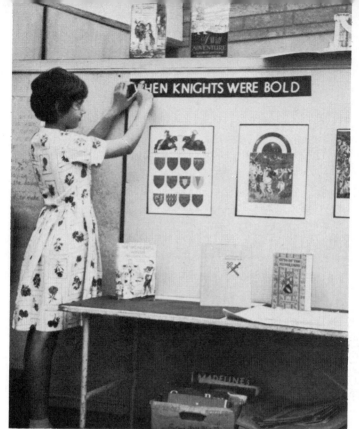

Figure 11–6.

Figure 11–7.

174

Figure 11–8.

Through the numerous activities in the library program, many of those participating learn some self-discipline; gain some knowledge of organization, punctuality, neatness, and efficiency; and some may possibly become librarians (Figures 11–6, 11–7, and 11–8). Others gain an insight into, and appreciation of, the busy activities going on behind the quiet front desk in the library.

One such program is presented in the following discussion:

The first step toward channeling the bubbling energy of enthusiastic library volunteers is to organize. Notices are posted in grades four, five, and six for the meeting after school in the library for all those interested in becoming library helpers.

At the first meeting, the librarian presents requirements and regulations:

1. Two after-school periods a week devoted to library work.
   a. One period for a group meeting.
   b. One period for carrying out routine duties.
2. Some members may prefer to work fifteen to thirty minutes each morning before school starts.

(*Note:* Length of working periods depends on the school and the group, but a 45–50 minute period seems best for good home-school relations.)

3. Procedures
   a. The assistant is on time.
   b. If the librarian is busy at check-in time, the assistant performs current jobs, such as reading shelves or shelving until he is assigned a specific job.
   c. The assistant works quietly.
   d. The office is off-limits unless the assistant is assigned to work there.
   e. At dismissal time, the assistant finishes the loose ends quickly and leaves without being reminded more than once.
   f. Three unexcused absences drop him from membership. If he is absent, he brings a note from home the day he returns. Forgetfulness or staying after school to make up class work are not acceptable excuses.
   g. Working at the desk, the assistant
      1) Checks for clean hands.
      2) Checks the overdue list.
      3) Is courteous at all times, turning problems over to the librarian.
      4) Keeps his voice low and does not talk any more than necessary.
      5) Serves one patron at a time and does not rush.
      6) Gives patron his books only after he checks the cards for correct signature and legibility.
      7) Stamps date slips and cards right side up in the proper column.
      8) If a card is filled, he paper clips old card and new card back to back before the patron signs.

4. Maintenance of at least a C grade in each basic subject because
   a. It is out of the question to take the child's time for library routines after school if his studies suffer as a result of the time loss.
   b. It is an incentive to improve in school work.
   c. A certain amount of success in school studies indicates the child can cope with library job routines. Time and again inefficiency and laxness have resulted when the opportunity is given to those not meeting the prerequisites.

At the end of the grading period the members show their cards to the librarian. They appreciate her interest in their other school activities. And they are encouraged, even if grades are in question, for a child may receive a leave of absence to have a chance to improve his academic work while still remaining in good standing in the library club.

    5. Written permission from the applicant's teacher and parents to participate. E.g.,

---

Dear Parents,

    .... would like to be a helper in the .... School Library this year. It means he would need to be available after school two days a week: Tuesday and one other day.

    Should you approve, please sign the statement below and return it to the librarian. Thank you.

                            Yours sincerely,

                          ....
                          Children's librarian

....

Yes, ... may help in the School Library after school two days a week: Tuesday and ....

....

Teacher's approval   Parent's signature

Those returning notices with the parents' and teachers' signatures showing approval of their participation in library activities after school meet the following week to plan the work program. The group is divided so there will be some helpers on each day other than the club meeting time.

Should the numbers of children still be too excessive for the librarian to work with, nevertheless, they are all accepted with enthusiasm. The field narrows down soon enough after the first two or three meetings to those who have a true interest in the library.

At the first two or three meetings, the librarian may give the group written drill on alphabetizing fiction authors and later enumerating Dewey numbers. Obviously the helpers will be shelving books. And such activity, which supplements the library instruction for classrooms, is important before the children are assigned jobs in shelving, putting daily circulation in order, filing, etc.

The written activity eliminates the need for correcting many errors that would occur otherwise in the assistants' work at the shelves or the desk. Some children at this time will automatically realize this really is not what they want to do in their after-school free time and will drop of their own accord. The librarian needs to plan activities well for those who remain, to avoid having children standing around waiting for job assignments.

One method is to have pockets labeled with one or two duties posted on a chart. The librarian places each assistant's card in one of the pockets to tell him immediately what routine job he is to perform. E.g., Willie and Debra find their cards in the pocket marked *desk.* This means they are on duty checking out books and putting the daily circulation in order. Each one briefly fills in his activity card with the date and duties performed, thus:

```
Willie Rowan            Grade 5
       9–25   circulation
       9–28   desk
       10–9   paste pockets
       10–19  circulation
       10–22  shelve fiction
```

An activity card assures the children of a variety of jobs.

On another posted chart containing the names of all members the librarian places blue stars. The stars represent the number of times each has served. After fifteen stars, a large green star may be added for each five additional times. This gives each member some idea of his services to his school community.

The services library assistants perform are many:

1. Charging books to patrons.
2. Putting daily circulation in order, counting and recording it, and interfiling it.
3. Double checking accession numbers of books checked in, before these go into circulation again.
4. Sorting and checking-in books.
5. Cutting bookmarks and other materials.
6. Assembling and stapling booklets or other materials for special occasions, such as Book Week.
7. Pasting pockets and stamping new books.
8. Arranging bulletin board displays.
9. Posting book jackets.
10. Preliminary sorting of books for shelving.
11. Shelving books.

12. Aligning books on the shelves.
13. Pulling catalog cards for withdrawals.
14. Alphabetizing new catalog cards.
15. Preliminary filing of catalog cards "above the rod."
16. Filing *National Geographic* pamphlets and vertical file material.
17. Pulling overdue cards and listing overdue notices.
18. Operating the viewing-listening center.

Common problems arising may be aired and cleared at a general meeting.

At the end of the first six weeks of library assistant activities, the members know each other well enough to elect officers. The president may be in charge of those wishing to contribute their services during noon browsing periods. In addition, there will be some social activities which he, a vice-president, and a secretary will direct.

The members volunteering for committee work are appointed by the president to help plan social activities with singing, book games, or variety shows. The librarian may do much indirect guidance on these, such as encouraging someone into giving a chalk talk. Sometimes such programs may spill over into a school assembly, or the library club "act" may be part of a larger school program.

Such activities are necessary occasionally to boost enthusiasm in any working group. At the end of the year, too, this group with the other service groups in the school may be given special recognition. E.g., at an awards assembly fourth graders may receive certificates; fifth and sixth graders, certificates or pins for the first year of service; and sixth graders, a guard to go with the pin earned in grade five.

However, there are other ways of showing appreciation for services rendered:

1. When new books have been processed, library assistants have first chance at reading them.
2. The librarian may take members to a stage production in the area, such as *Rumplestiltskin, Amahl and the Night Visitors,* or *Winnie the Pooh.*
3. The club members may visit a printing shop. Private printing plants where type is hand-set and machines manually run are fascinating to children.
4. A popular, rewarding activity each year is in the field of communications. Those who turn in a reference report on the subject make paper from pressed wood pulp or papyrus, and clay or wax tablets. Children with artistic ability may enjoy working out an il-

lustrated manuscript page. These projects are limited to a small group such as the library club. (As class projects, they would be classroom activities correlated to units of study.)

5. The librarian who is a camera bug may take pictures or films of various phases of the library assistants' program. These may be shown to the whole school, to the PTA, or other interested groups.

The library assistants' program is obviously a varied and valuable part of the school curriculum.

Chapter 12—

Challenging Horizons—

Preparing for An Expanded Library

Marie Grieco, lecturer at the Columbia University Graduate School of Library Science, states,[1] "If there is a 'keynote,' if there is a prescription, here it is: a state of mind, an attitude toward education, an approach to learning, an understanding of media, a concept of communication, all of which has to do with perception and with people."

Communities are beginning to hear the keynote and are taking heed. No longer does the elementary school library only circulate books and act as a storehouse for a-v equipment and perhaps a limited supply of flash cards and other such media. These are no longer just checked out for classroom use and returned to the library for storage. The time has finally arrived when the library also has become a user of these materials—for instruction, story hour, and general use.

An audio-visual center today is looked upon as a permanent part of the elementary school library. Checking out records and other audio-visuals to children is the practice followed in schools with sufficient funds to maintain such materials. Although printed books or those on microfilm may continue to be the core of the library, records, filmstrips, transparencies, and other multi-media are becoming an essential part of the collection used both in the library and

---

[1] In her article *Communications . . . The Undiscovered Country* (*School Library Journal*, February, 1967, p. 32).

in the classrooms. No one medium is necessarily the best. Children react differently and learn, each according to his own make-up. So, having many media available will serve to meet these different minds and individual needs.

In retrospect, beyond the picture of the library as a storehouse for audio-visual equipment, the view takes one back to the time when only pictures were the "extras" to check out along with books. To be sure, the picture file is still a standard library audio-visual item. Bulging vertical files are active witnesses to its importance in library circulation (Figure 12–1). School librarians have constantly striven to keep the file currently correlated to the curriculum. Library budgets have to a limited extent provided for pictures, though in many libraries the bulk of the file comes from home magazines and various free sources.

Added to these vertical file materials are large prints of master-pieces of art, oversized charts for science and other subjects, and transparencies. Many schools receive these on loan from a central district or county a-v center.

Figure 12–1.

The "keynote" has reached many districts, for many elementary school libraries now receive budgets exclusively for the purchase of pictures, records, filmstrips, and transparencies. These budgets, though increased by federal funds, are now beginning to parallel book budgets and may even exceed them.

The school needs appropriate equipment in order to utilize audio-visuals: motion picture, filmstrip, opaque, and overhead projectors; record players, and tape recorders. School districts face constant difficulties in this area because

1. Equipment is expensive.
2. Maintenance is a problem.
3. Training of personnel is inadequate.
4. Availability of machines when needed can be a great obstacle where circulation occurs from a central point.

All these problems need to be met and solved with the cooperation of the administration, the classroom teachers, and the librarian. Expensive audio-visuals are often provided for general classroom use. Having the equipment, however, and even resolving the above problems do not insure its use; it is worthless unless the teacher is sold on its value in teaching the disciplines of subject matter. It is of little value unless it becomes an integral part of communication in the education of the child. To be fully integrated, the various media of communication need to be extended also into the elementary school library itself where a listening-and-viewing center with carrels are available for reference and leisure time activities.

Those schools in the planning stage are incorporating a-v centers into their blueprints. Elementary school libraries fortunate enough to be looking toward expansion are including these centers. But, many elementary school libraries simply do not have space available within the library to install such facilities. How to surmount this first provision is a real challenge. The forward-looking librarian with determination will find a way.

With careful planning and adjustment of space, it is possible to squeeze out areas for the use of a-v equipment (Figure 12–2). Children might crowd a small textbook room for the viewmasters and a workroom corner where an electrical outlet is handy for the filmstrip viewer. As illustrated in Figures 12–3 and 12–4, several children wearing headphones may use a table in one corner of the library to hear "Babes In Toyland" or "The Sorcerer's Apprentice." Several

Figure 12–2.

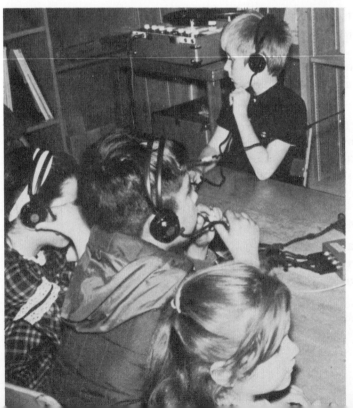

Figure 12–3.

Figure 12–4.

pupils, including the primaries, who have been taught to operate the machines, also remind the children of proper handling of equipment.

Earlier, during its scheduled library time, the librarian has instructed each class in the proper use of the a-v center: e.g., in listening to records:

Keep fingers off the receiving part of the headphones.
Adjust the size of the headphones.
Keep the cord free and uncrossed.
Roll up the cord and lay the phones next to the junction box.[2]
Do not handle the phonograph unless you're trained and appointed. Turning the volume button could permanently damage the listener's hearing.

Directions may be posted to guide the child, though he will still need initial directions from the librarian or another teacher, and some supervision.

---

[2] This is only one type, of course, for with others the cords automatically slide into a boxed unit when not in use.

Figure 12–5.

A trained operator may instruct primary children in the use of view-masters and reels, demonstrating how to handle the reel to avoid smudging the film. (See Figure 12–5.) He may also run the individual filmstrip machine for the child having difficulty in threading or rewinding the filmstrip. Where space allows, he may run the large filmstrip projector for general viewing. Tape recorders may be operated in like manner. The instruction in the operation of these occurs in both the classroom and the library where there is no a-v coordinator in the school.

Management, organization, and instruction in a-v activities take time. Where personnel is below the standards in number and in training, the challenge may be almost overwhelming. But Miss Grieco, on p. 33 of her article mentioned above, also states ". . . facilities alone do not insure services, and collections alone do not insure optimal use." Until sufficient staffing occurs, it will take a dedicated librarian with tremendous perseverance to surmount the obstacles as she is concurrently besieged with requests for help in book selection, reference, and from time to time some irrelevant matters!

The constant demand to use a make-shift a-v center testifies to its popularity, value, and need. It is a learning center not just for the culturally disadvantaged and the child with a reading handicap, but for *all* children.

These multi-media will meet the needs of many disadvantaged children. As an example, for an oral report the fifth or sixth grader unable to use reference tools such as encyclopedias because of severe reading problems might well make use of a handviewer and a filmstrip or a record or tape.

Or, the gifted workshop may fully round out each unit of work with multi-media. Should they begin a study of buildings of antiquity, the children will explore all possible familiar sources in the library: *Picturesque Tale of Progress,* trade books, vertical file, the unabridged dictionary, periodicals, encyclopedias, and end with the *Lincoln Library* for the specific dimensions of the Parthenon, the Sphinx, etc. But not until they see the building on a VM reel or on a filmstrip does the book learning begin to take shape and form for them. And their enthusiasm becomes boundless when they see colored motion pictures of the particular building which the librarian has taken on her travels.

A strand of human hair or the stinger of a bumble bee under a microscope creates a long line of viewers. One needs to be willing to start with *one* microscope. Classrooms gladly reinforce this or *vice versa.* Seeing a microscopic view of the leg of a housefly or a drop of water can do more than weeks of talking in the classroom to make children aware of filth and disease and start them thinking about the prevention of these! Such an a-v medium may lead many a child to the library books on experiments with the microscope or books on the particular subject. Such a stimulus can also be the beginning of a budding scientist.

Among other audio-visuals, records on foreign languages, arithmetic, music, fairy tales, and other stories are essential to a viewing-listening center. Children clamor to be allowed to use the headphones. An appropriate space and place in the library needs to be provided for children to listen to such fine recordings as *The Frog and The Flea* narrated by artists Ruth Sawyer and Francis Clarke Sayers.

Children have strong desires to hear or view the same material over and over. They listen repeatedly, e.g., to *Johnny Appleseed* as they view the pictures that are part of the album. They enjoy the combination of record and filmstrip, such as *The Firebird.* And, they listen to the sounds of game and domestic birds while they view pictures of the fowl. Like a good or useful book, audio-visuals are used again and again, often by the same individuals. Having these easily accessible for the children is not easy to achieve but is the view of the library of the future.

Once a school has achieved the first goals of having audio-visuals in the collection and making these easily available for classroom and home use, the next problem is how and where to house them. This and the second point above are, to be sure, inseparable for optimum use of the collection. Placing records and filmstrips on the shelf with books all on the same subject, e.g., is the desirable pattern. Using color-banded cards may help resolve the problem of cataloging these materials. The cards can then be interfiled in the dictionary catalog or separately. Obviously, it is necessary to have sufficient personnel to complete the cataloging with all the desirable cross-referencing.

The audio-visuals with the equipment circulate into the class-rooms. Checking out records, filmstrips, etc., for classroom use is a simple process. It is the transportation of equipment that is the problem. Small children cannot handle it properly even by cart. No matter where it is housed, teachers do not have the time to run it back and forth. Nor does the librarian, who in her own right is a full-fledged teacher, have time to do this. But use of these is essential for adequate correlation and integration of learning and worthy use of leisure time by the child.

But an initial effort, with the temporary make-shift set-up in a library as discussed above, is the first important step. Once the effort is made, the desire and need are established for both classroom use and library use. Almost automatically a greater number of machines for permanent use on grade levels is made available, and the circulation of records and other audio-visuals increases.

As in other classroom teaching, audio-visuals are effective as a tool in library instruction. The children passing through our schools to-day belong to a generation saturated with television. From their earliest days they have been accustomed to viewing a picture on a screen, accompanied by sound effects of some sort. To them this is a natural way of learning rather than listening to an adult expatiate on a given subject. There is apparently a correlation in the minds of many children between teacher talking and parent nagging, and as soon as the teacher opens her mouth the class turns down its hearing aids. The audio-visuals for teaching library skills therefore are one means of overcoming this.

Today there is no excuse for not incorporating different types of audio-visuals into library instruction. An opaque projector, where pages and illustrations may be produced directly from a book, is an excellent device for a small group in a room which can be completely darkened. For a large group, an overhead projector is highly effective. A great advantage of this latter is it is not necessary to have a darkened room.

Good transparencies may be purchased but it is possible to have desired material made up within a school district. The results of a grease pencil on a roll of acetate threaded through the machine have greater appeal and are easier to view than material presented on a chalkboard. There are innumerable filmstrips and many motion pictures which add variety and interest to the program of library instruction.

Some of these may be for instructing children in the manipulating of a-v equipment. A quick after-school workshop on a new piece of equipment is not enough for teachers. Unless they take an a-v course, they become frustrated. The pressure of time often makes them use force on equipment which winds up in the repair shop. Children with their minds free from cares and worries which constantly harass the classroom teacher can easily and quickly absorb the mechanics of operating simple machinery. Experience has proved that with well-trained juvenile operators, a-v equipment remains in good running condition longer! In addition, the teacher is freed to give attention to the concepts she is teaching.

Many types of multi-media have been mentioned in this book. Motion pictures, filmstrips, records, pictures, slides, flannelboards, realia such as a real American Indian skull and other visual devices like the Dewey wheel become a natural part of the library curriculum. The old saying about one picture being worth ten thousand words in a learning situation can be expanded to "one filmstrip may very well be worth a dozen or more books on the same subject!"

The librarian and the classroom teacher exercise their ingenuity in using these tools and integrating them into classroom curriculum. The Dewey wheel, the giant cards used to teach the card catalog, and other such materials may be borrowed for supportive classroom instruction, such as in the concentrated library program. Clay tablets made by library club members can be checked out to fit into a communications project or other unit in the classroom. It has happened that an eighth grader returned to her first school to borrow clay tablets made when she had been in library club there four years before!

Also available for classroom reinforcement of the library instruction are the transparencies and filmstrips on encyclopedias, almanacs, yearbooks, and other reference tools. The librarian and the teacher, working closely together, correlate the library instruction with the units of study in the classroom. E.g., a sixth grade beginning a unit on maps or globes in September means the librarian will temporarily dismiss any thoughts of lessons on the Dewey Decimal System and filing cards. She plans instead lessons on the available library materials on maps and globes. The class becomes acquainted with the atlases in the library, learning about their differences and likenesses and the main features of each. Transparencies and filmstrips reinforce the study of atlases: the use of the index, the different types of maps, legends, and the information in each type of atlas. Mercator, equal-area, and polar maps are defined, illustrated, and discussed. The librarian gives specific lessons on how to read maps and globes; the classroom teacher reviews these and the children apply their learning through classroom assignments. They may produce their own visual materials, transparencies, relief maps, etc.

Another far-reaching and stimulating aspect of audio-visuals could be an exhibit case with a taped commentary on the display—very like the a-v "set-ups" in large zoos. Even a fairly small exhibit case could be effective, especially with change of displays as often as feasible. The child turns on the tape or pushes a button to hear the commentary on the display. It is a potentially powerful communications center.

The library is no longer just a storehouse for books and pictures since it has added many multi-media easily accessible for school and home use. These, like books, are disseminators of information, and they serve for relaxation and enjoyment.

These new methods of communication may resolve the perplexing problem of how to give background material in library skills— and surely classroom studies—to a child coming into the school during the course of the year, to one who is absent during the discussion of a skill, or to a slow learner. The librarian or teacher from unit to unit records on tape the lessons covered and the newcomer wearing headphones hears these in the library. Or, he may view the transparencies that are listed for the particular skill. And he may want to check these out overnight for home use and later talk over the trouble spots with the librarian or teacher.

No longer does the child need to rely solely on a book. The important point is that he has the opportunity to gain his knowledge from many different sources: trade books, the reference tools, periodicals, tapes, motion pictures, filmstrips, records, microfilm, etc. Any medium "goes" as long as the child learns. And when libraries begin to make many media easily available for home use, the whole family can benefit from a child's home work or home leisure enjoyment.

Thus far no mention has been made of the use of automation in retrieving information for the child in the elementary school. The possibility is there but may be long in coming. Currently, so many elementary schools do not even have libraries that the idea of just having a collection of books would be a miracle.

Meanwhile, schools are adding or expanding their audio-visual collections. This is real.

Because of its accessibility and convenience for the whole school, the school library needs to be able to readily handle and check out audio-visuals.[3] It can well follow the practice of many public libraries in providing satchels or other means for protecting and easy handling of multi-media. And having mother or father pick up the equipment entices the whole family in the learning process.

Thus, audio-visuals and equipment for running them in a convenient listening-and-viewing center and making them available for check-out have as important a role in the library program as do books when they open new worlds of joy and enchantment, security, and knowledge to the child.

---

[3] Two references among the best on this subject are H. M. McLuhan, *Understanding Media.* (McGraw, New York, 1964.) Paperback. *School Library Journal.* Vol. 13, no. 6, Feb., 1967, Audio-visual issue.

Chapter 13—

Old Wine in New Bottles—

Flexible Scheduling for
Library Skills Instruction

All teachers find that many hours of instruction are filled with frustration, with trial and error, and with the application of the old saw: "If at first you don't succeed . . ." The lesson that was so successful with last year's sixth grade leaves this year's unmoved; the story that this year's fifth graders laugh over hilariously will fall like a lead balloon on next year's fifth grade.

The same is true in the teaching of library skills. There is no one method that can be guaranteed to be always successful. Guidelines can be laid down, but there are many ways of elaborating on these. Each lesson is really an adjustment to all the delicate balances and subtle nuances that make up a corporate class. The librarian's situation is a very challenging one since she deals with all grade levels from kindergarten through sixth grade, and ultimately with every class in the school. Her day is made up of adjustments.

There is, of course, a time pattern set up in each school for instruction in library skills, and each librarian will need to use this time block to the best advantage from the point of view of the over-all school curriculum. The following discussion refers to elementary schools with full-time or at least half-time professional librarians. Here the traditional pattern has been for a weekly visitation of each class involved. The time usually varies from thirty minutes for the younger children to fifty minutes for the older ones. Although children are free to browse at other times during the day, often a portion of the scheduled period is given over to book selection, further curtailing the instructional time. In many instances formal instruction does not start until the fourth grade, though it is hoped the discussion in this book has revealed that much younger children can adequately absorb many library skills.

One of the results of this pattern is an extremely diluted library skills program. It is seldom possible to cover the amount of material that the librarian considers desirable. Elementary school children do not have the maturity or training to retain details of instruction when there is a lapse of seven days. Each week's lesson needs to be introduced with a review and drill of the previous week's material. Possibly two or three new points may be introduced, which, again at the next visit must be carefully repeated. With this constant repetition the progress, even with an academically advanced class, creeps along at a snail's pace. Both librarian and children often become weary of a dragging unit before it has been digested. The necessity for a different approach is evident.

CONCENTRATED INSTRUCTION

A variation from the diluted or diffused program is the concentrated library program. It surmounts the above-mentioned difficulties, though it may give rise to other problems, which each librarian will need to resolve according to her own school situation.

One satisfactory pattern for a concentrated library program is

1. Kindergarten through second grades do not come to the library for instruction during the first half of the year, as they do in the conventional or traditional program described in Chapter 1. *But,* in the spring, the librarian is freed to work closely with these grades on frequently scheduled visits.
2. The traditional approach is continued for grades three and four,[1] with one lesson period a week for each section throughout the year.

All formal instruction is concluded at the end of the first half year for the grades involved in the concentrated program. Although the library has been accessible for reference work during this time, con-

---

[1] Some fourth grade classes are mature enough for concentrated instruction; some are not. This also applies to large-group instruction.

centrated application of skills learned in the fall comes in the spring through reference assignments.

In a small school it is possible to work with individual classes in such a program. This is an ideal arrangement because:

1. Instruction may then occur in the library.
2. All necessary materials for demonstration are at hand.
3. Reference tools, etc., are in their familiar places.
4. Other students may use the library for reference or browsing during this time.[2]
5. Drill work, such as reading non-fiction shelves, filing catalog cards, etc., is easy to administer.
6. The librarian and teacher can give much individual guidance in library instruction.
7. Less time is lost for a small group to assemble for instruction.

Although the concentrated program takes a large block of time from the classroom program—and the effects of this are more noticeable in departmentalized programming—the loss to classroom work in the fall will balance out in the spring.

LARGE-GROUP INSTRUCTION

A real problem of the traditional program is the inordinate amount of time consumed because each class is individually scheduled. In a large elementary school, with several sections of each grade, there is not time in the week's schedule to accommodate both primary and upper grade children adequately and still allow reasonable blocks of time (30 to 50 minutes) for reference work.

To compensate for this, another aspect of instruction which librarians may find worth exploring is the method of large-group instruction where all sections of each grade involved meet together as a group[3] for a half-hour of library instruction, based on a lecture-

---

[2] Some state laws, such as California's, require an adult to be present in any room being used by children.

[3] Two schools in the Shaker Heights, Ohio, School District have worked with large-group instruction. This is considered a successful program and is one that was heavily undergirded financially. The authors have experimented with both concentrated and large-group instruction programs within the regular framework of the district library program, and with no additional financial support or personnel.

type approach. For book selection each individual section of all grades involved comes to the library for another period during the week.

This large-group instruction may take place over the *entire year* with each grade level meeting *once a week*. Or, it may be *concentrated* into the first half of the year, in which case each grade will need to meet twice a week plus a third period for book selection as noted above.

When large-group instruction is used on a concentrated basis, it is necessary to work out a satisfactory arrangement timewise between teacher and librarian which will allow students to perform "laboratory" exercises in the library, under the supervision of the librarian.

The most constantly voiced criticism of the concentrated and/or large-group instruction program is that too many children will not absorb the information. In any teaching situation, there is a small group lost because the children do not listen or are not mentally equipped to absorb the material. The percentage does not seem to be necessarily greater in concentrated or large-group instruction, though the children thus affected may be different from those in a small group. Some children respond better in larger groups where a giant screen, a microphone, and a darkened room are used. Grasp of knowledge depends on how the learning situation affects the individual child.

SUMMARY

The advantages and disadvantages of a concentrated and/or large-group instruction program are:

Advantages	*Disadvantages*
1. Better use of time in the overall school library program.	1. Little or no flexibility in the program.
2. Less repetition of previous lesson; hence, greater coverage of material and greater possibility of achieving goals set.	2. Not feasible for librarian and teacher to meet often enough to create as effective a correlation between the classroom and the library due to pressures from daily routines.
3. Learning and retention are greater.	

Advantages	*Disadvantages*

4. A more conscientious and cooperative faculty and administration. Teachers feel a responsibility to participate in the program.
5. Many teachers are learning library skills too and
   A. Become aware of the problems confronting the children in library usage.
   B. Are much more aware of ways the library can enrich classroom studies, making for a greater correlation between library instruction and classroom studies.
6. Greater continuity from week to week.
   E.g., under the traditional method when the class loses a period because of an assembly or for testing, etc., the class may go for several weeks without a library period.
7. Training in reference skills and tools the first semester means opportunity and time for intelligent application of these the entire second semester, and so a better retention for the following years.
8. Children can gain skill in notetaking because the presentation needs to be carefully organized and very direct and clear.

3. The instruction loses somewhat through the lack of library environment since large-group instruction will normally be held in a multipurpose room or other large area.
4. Audio-visual materials are not always available when needed and requested from a standard source.
5. Conflicts occur on availability of a room other than the library. This disrupts
   A. Sequence of instruction in a necessarily closely planned schedule.
   B. Scheduled audio-visual aids.
6. The librarian may lose the personal touch in large-group instruction.
7. It is not possible to give individual guidance except in laboratory work.
8. Other library matters may suffer the first semester. There is less time for book reviews, story-telling, and divergencies which make for greater interest in the library program.

This is a program which needs to be exactly planned, according to the time available. It is only with time and practice that a librarian acquires skill in such planning. For this reason and those discussed below the librarian new to the field will not immediately want to attempt a concentrated and/or large-group instruction program.

1. A librarian needs experience in teaching library skills in order to know what points and ideas to stress and which ones to pass over lightly.

2. It takes considerable practice to organize a lesson to the exact time available.

3. A librarian needs to know the children—by name, preferably —knowledge which comes only after several years of working in a school. Nothing is quite so effective in getting a child's attention in a large-group situation as to hear his name boom out over the microphone.

4. The need for the closest cooperation between teachers and the librarian cannot be too strongly emphasized. Such a program can rise or fall depending on the strength or weakness of the team teaching. A librarian new to a school, with all the good will in the world, does not have this rapport until she has lived for a while with the staff. The librarian needs to prove herself both to her teaching colleagues and to her principal before she is accorded positive and active support in an innovative program.

5. The program requires many audio-visual aids which a new librarian needs to become acquainted with. She will want to acquire skill in handling them before she attempts the program.

6. It is not practical to think anyone can hold the attention of a large group of elementary school children for half an hour by discussing a library skill over a microphone. Each lesson needs to be supported by one or more audio-visual aids—transparencies, filmstrips, movies, recordings. All these need to be previewed and evaluated before being put to use, a monumental task for the new librarian.

7. Accompanying each unit are:
   a. An information sheet reinforcing the instruction on the library skill.
   b. One or more worksheets done by the children in the classroom under the teacher's direction.
   c. A "laboratory" exercise done in the library during reference periods under the direction of the librarian.

It takes several years of experimenting to work out really satisfactory exercises which elicit the information the librarian has attempted to emphasize.

These, then, are two possibilities for breaking through the traditional methods of presenting library skills. As the librarian becomes more secure in her school environment, she may want to experiment with other patterns. The adventuresome librarian will find new methods of instruction one of the most challenging aspects of her daily round.

Chapter 14—

Assembling the Flotsam and Jetsam—

Making the Job

Easier

Tote Boxes

Each tote box contains sixty or more books for second grade reading levels. These are in addition to classroom collections chosen by the teacher and to books chosen by the class during its regular library visit. In addition to the classroom collection, these tote box books go home with the children.

Book cards for the tote box collections may be kept in separate packs tagged with the teachers' names. The books go to the classroom each with a tagboard card, labeled with author and title, in the pocket of the book. The children thus have their own little classroom library for checking books in and out.

When the box is returned to the library, the circulation figures are counted from these tagboard cards and may be added to the regular library circulation figures for the year.

Teachers may exchange tote boxes during the semester. The second grade tote boxes are replaced with a more advanced collection. The librarian sends the original boxes from the second grades to the first grades, with additional grade one reading level titles replacing the grade three books.

Record Collection Storage

The district shop or the school custodian can usually make an adequate case for the record collection of the elementary school. This is not apt to be so large that it cannot be fitted into some corner of the library. Filmstrips, many of which can be produced by the children themselves, and what films the school may own, can be stored in drawers, or in a small section of the shelving. Shelving records and filmstrips by subject on the shelves alongside the books is the ideal arrangement. Transparencies fit comfortably into a vertical file. Separate card catalogs may be maintained for each of these materials, or color coded cards may be interfiled into the main card catalog.

TOOLS FOR TEACHING

Chapter 1. Beginning Activities for Each Grade

    a. Sample book cards are made and cut to normal size on ditto paper for practice in signing one's name in preparation for checking out books.
    b. Labels to be used on the tagboard blueprint of the library are cut out of various colored construction paper and printed with India ink.

Chapter 2. How to Teach Alphabetizing

    a. A B C flash cards are large squares of white cardboard, the letters inked in with a broad, black felt pen so each letter is plainly seen across the room.
    b. Packs of dittoed cards with authors' names can be assembled by library helpers.
    c. Sheets of samples duplicating book spines can be assembled by library helpers.
    d. Packs of 3 x 5 author, title, and subject cards can be assembled thus, too.

Chapter 7. Learning the Dewey Decimal System

    a. The Dewey Decimal wheel, designed to help in the understanding of the Dewey Decimal System, was developed by the authors. (See Figure 14–1.)

DEWEY DECIMAL WHEEL

2 frames with as many inner wheels as desired

hole or hinge

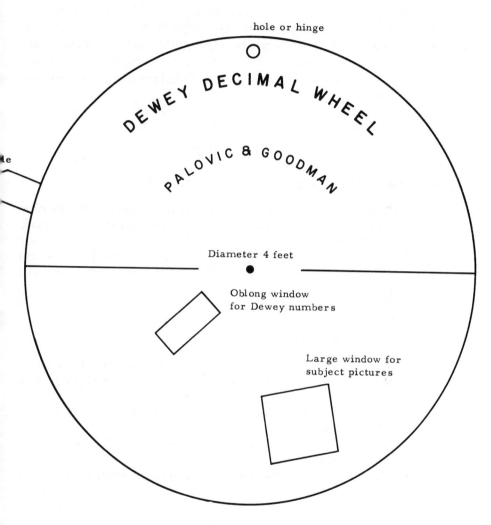

DEWEY DECIMAL WHEEL

PALOVIC & GOODMAN

Diameter 4 feet

Oblong window
for Dewey numbers

Large window for
subject pictures

Object of the game: To name the subject for the Dewey number appearing
in the window, or to name the Dewey classification number for
the subject picture appearing in the large window.

Figure 14–1.

DEWEY DECIMAL WHEEL*

Frame: two wheels made of fine, durable plastic or other durable synthetic material, bolted together at the center so they may revolve . . . four feet in diameter. The wheels could be hinged across the center for folding to facilitate mailing and transportation.

A short durable *handle* to twirl or spin the outer frame—one on each side, so both sides may be used.

A hole or *hinge* on each outer frame so the wheel may be hung in full view of the class.

TWO WINDOWS on each frame: *Larger* one to show *subject pictures* on outer circle. Smaller, oblong one to show Dewey decimal numbers on inner circle.

Inner Wheels: Any number of these, but only one used at any one time: These contain *subject pictures* that appear in the window when the spinning frame stops; Dewey *numbers* appear in the *oblong window* when the spinning frame stops.

The numbers and subject pictures do *not* go together. The player has a choice.

   Examples:

   Wheel one: *Side one* contains subject pictures representing the ten
      Dewey classes and five or more of the class numbers, as illustrated
      on the enclosed example.

   Side two contains various subject pictures and other Dewey class
      numbers to complete or supplement side one.

   Wheel two: *Subdivisions* of one class such as subject pictures for
      side one:

mathematics	trees	weather
dinosauria	chemistry	birds
astronomy	reptiles	animals
		shells

   and in the *oblong window* would appear for example:

   398   973   220   970.1   636

   Side two: Subject pictures of any other class or a mixture, along
      with various numbers such as

   780   387   627   812   460

Additional wheels would cover any subjects or Dewey numbers; some could be set up according to grade levels.

---

* The object of the game is for the group to name the Dewey number for the subject picture shown. Or, to name the subject of the number appearing in the oblong window.

b. *Mr. Dewey's Naughty Boy*

700 .... art		629.14 .... airplanes
398 .... folk tales		371.33 .... lecture
332.4 ..... money		972 .... Mexico
685.3 ..... shoes		970.1 ..... Indian
552 .... rocks		790 .... fun
582.17 .... shrubs		812 .... plays
540 .... chemistry		523 .... sun
796.357 ... baseball		910 .... travel
797.2 ..... swimming		749 .... furniture
621.388 ... television		666.1 ..... glassware
423 .... English		951 .... China
796 .... sport		395 .... manners
513 .... geometry		636.2 ..... cow
737 .... coin		921 .... biography
537 .... electricity		364.36 .... juvenile delinquent
947 .... Russia ("rush yah")		930 .... ancient history
786.2 ..... piano		

Chapter 8. The Card Catalog

a. The tagboard strips for lessons on the catalog cards are labeled with each item on a separate strip; author, title twice, publisher, copyright date, page numbers, illustrations, call number, and subject. The children arrange these on the flannelboard in correct order.

b. For the lesson making author, title, and subject cards, the slips of paper are cut to the size of the standard catalog card. Or, practice cards may be bought from library supply houses.

Appendix I

Titles Cited in the

Text

Newbery Medal Books and Caldecott Medal Books are listed separately. Atlases, dictionaries and encyclopedias are also listed separately.

Louisa May Alcott, *Little Men* (New York: Grosset & Dunlap, Publishers, 1947).

Louisa May Alcott, *Little Women* (New York: Grosset & Dunlap, Publishers, 1947).

Louisa May Alcott, *An Old Fashioned Girl* (Cleveland: The World Publishing Company, 1947).

Louisa May Alcott, *Rose in Bloom* (Boston: Little, Brown, and Company, 1951).

Agnes Allen, *The Story of the Book* (London: Faber and Faber, 1952).

American Association of School Librarians, *Standards for School Library Programs* (Chicago: American Library Association, 1960).

A Basic Book Collection for Elementary Grades (Chicago: American Library Association, 1960).

C. W. Anderson, *A Filly for Joan* (New York: The Macmillan Company, 1960).

Barbara K. Anthony, *Explorers All* (Grand Rapids, Michigan: Fideler Company, 1942).

May Hill Arbuthnot, comp., *Time for Fairy Tales, Old and New* (Chicago: Scott, Foresman and Company, 1952).

P. C. Asbjønsen and J. E. Moe, *East O' the Sun and West O' the Moon* (Garden City, New York: Junior DeLuxe Editions, 1957).

Ingri and Edgar Parin d'Aulaire, *Buffalo Bill* (Garden City, New York: Doubleday & Company, Inc., 1952).

"Away-She-Go," in Maynard Dixon, *Injun Babies* (New York: G. P. Putnam's Sons, 1923).

Rachel Baker, *The First Woman Doctor* (New York: Julian Messner, Inc., 1944).

George Barr, *Research Ideas for Young Scientists* (New York: Whittlesey House, 1958).

J. M. Barrie, *Peter Pan* (New York: Charles Scribner's Sons, 1950).

John Bartlett, *Familiar Quotations* (Boston: Little, Brown and Company, 1955).

Julie Forsyth Batchelor, *A Cap for Mul Chand* (New York: Harcourt, Brace & World, Inc., 1950).

Julie Forsyth Batchelor, *Communication: From Cave Writing to Television* (New York: Harcourt, Brace & World, Inc., 1953).

L. Frank Baum, *The Wizard of Oz* (New York: Grosset & Dunlap, Inc., 1956).

Jeanne Bendick, *The First Book of Airplanes* (Boston: D. C. Heath and Company, 1952).

Margery Williams Bianco, *The Little Wooden Doll* (New York: The Macmillan Company, 1925).

John E. and Sara W. Brewton, comp., *Index to Children's Poetry* (New York: The H. W. Wilson Company, 1942).

Judith Gwyn Brown, *The Happy Voyage* (New York: The Macmillan Company, 1965).

Margaret Wise Brown, *The Runaway Bunny* (New York: Harper & Brothers, 1942).

"Budulinek," in Parker Fillmore, *Shoemaker's Apron* (New York: Harcourt, Brace & Company, Inc., 1920).

Mary and Conrad Buff, *The Apple and the Arrow* (Boston: Houghton Mifflin Company, 1951).

Clyde Robert Bulla, *The Sword in the Tree* (New York: Thomas Y. Crowell Company, 1956).

Mary June Burton, *Louis Pasteur, Founder of Microbiology* (New York: Franklin Watts, Inc., 1963).

Virginia Lee Burton, *Mike Mulligan and His Steam Shovel* (Boston: Houghton Mifflin Company, 1939).

Rhys Carpenter, et al, *Everyday Life in Ancient Times* (Washington, D.C.: The National Geographic Society, 1961).

Lewis Carroll, *Alice in Wonderland and Through the Looking Glass* (New York: Grosset & Dunlap, Publishers, 1946).

"The Cat and the Parrot," in W. Crooke, comp., *The Talking Thrush* (New York: E. P. Dutton & Company, Inc., 1938).

Alfred J. Church, *The Iliad for Boys and Girls Told from Homer in Simple Language* (New York: The Macmillan Company, 1935).

G. Glenwood Clark, *Thomas Alva Edison* (New York: Aladdin Books, 1951).

Beverly Cleary, *Henry Huggins* (New York: William Morrow & Company, 1950).

"Clever Manka," in Phyllis R. Fenner, *Fools and Funny Fellows* (New York: Alfred A. Knopf, Inc., 1947).

Catherine Cate Coblentz, *Ah-yo-Ka, Daughter of Sequoia* (Evanston, Illinois: Row, Peterson & Company, 1950).

C. Collodi, *The Adventures of Pinocchio* (New York: Grosset & Dunlap, Publishers, 1946).

Dorothy Berliner Commins, *Making an Orchestra* (New York: The Macmillan Company, 1931).

David Coxe Cooke, *How Books Are Made* (New York: Dodd, Mead & Company, Inc., 1963).

Ellis Credle, *Down Down the Mountain* (New York: Thomas Nelson & Sons, 1934).

W. Crooke, comp., *The Talking Thrush* (New York: E. P. Dutton & Company, Inc., 1938).

Alice Dalgliesh, *Ride on the Wind, Told by Alice Dalgliesh from The Spirit of St. Louis by Charles A. Lindbergh* (New York: Charles Scribner's Sons, 1956).

Clive E. Davis, *Man and Space* (New York: Dodd, Mead & Company, Inc., 1960).

Marguerite de Angeli, *Elin's Amerika* (Garden City, New York: Doubleday & Company, Inc., 1941).

Daniel Defoe, *Life and Adventures of Robinson Crusoe* (Cleveland: The World Publishing Company, 1946).

Etta DeGering, *Seeing Fingers* (New York: David McKay Company, Inc., 1962).

Aubrey De Sélincourt, *Odysseus the Wanderer* (New York: Criterion Books, Inc., 1956).

Melvil Dewey, *Dewey Decimal Classification and Relative Index,* ed. 17 (New York: Forest Press, Inc., of Lake Placid Club Education Foundation, 1965).

David Diringer, *Writing* (New York: F. A. Praeger, 1952).

Maynard Dixon, *Injun Babies* (New York: G. P. Putnam's Sons, 1923).

George William Douglas, *American Book of Days,* rev. by Helen Douglas Compton (New York: The H. W. Wilson Company, 1948).

Mary K. Eakin and Eleanor Merritt, comp., *Subject Index to Books for Primary Grades* (Chicago: American Library Association, 1961).

Mary Huse Eastman, *Index to Fairy Tales, Myths, and Legends* (Boston: The F. W. Faxon Company, 1926). *Supplement,* 1937; *Second Supplement,* 1952.

Irmengarde Eberle, *Benjamin Franklin, Man of Science* (New York: Franklin Watts, Inc., 1961).

Anne Emery, *Joan of Arc* (Evanston, Illinois: Row, Peterson and Company, 1951).

Sam and Beryl Epstein, *The First Book of Words, Their Family Histories* (Boston: D. C. Heath and Company, 1954).

Henry R. Fea, *Adventure in the Sierras* (Boston: Ginn & Company, 1959).

Phyllis R. Fenner, *Fools and Funny Fellows* (New York: Alfred A. Knopf, Inc., 1947).

Phyllis R. Fenner, *With Might and Main* (New York: Alfred A. Knopf, 1948).

Parker Fillmore, *Shoemaker's Apron* (New York: Harcourt, Brace & Company, 1920).

Marjorie Flack, *The Story of Ping* (New York: The Viking Press, 1933).

Franklin Folsom, *The Language Book* (New York: Grosset & Dunlap, Inc., 1963).

Harry Emerson Fosdick, *Martin Luther* (New York: Random House, Inc., 1956).

Joanna Foster, *Pages, Pictures, and Print* (New York: Harcourt, Brace & World, 1958).

Charles Philip Fox, *Mr. Duck's Big Day* (Chicago: Reilly & Lee, 1963).

"From Tiger to Anansi," in Philip M. Sherlock, *Anansi the Spider Man* (New York: Thomas Y. Crowell Company, 1954).

Muriel Fuller, ed., *More Junior Authors* (New York: The H. W. Wilson Company, 1963).

Wanda Gag, *The A B C Bunny* (New York: Coward-McCann, Inc., 1933).

Wanda Gag, *Millions of Cats* (New York: Coward-McCann, Inc., 1928).

Helen Gaspard, *Dr. Dan the Bandage Man* (New York: Simon and Schuster, 1950).

"The Gingerbread Man," in Olive Beaupré Miller, ed., *My Book House, Vol. II: Story Time* (Chicago: Book House for Children, 1950).

Fred Gipson, *Old Yeller* (New York: Harper & Brothers, 1956).

Kate Greenaway, *A Apple Pie* (New York: Frederick Warne & Company, Inc., 1886).

W. Cabell Greet, *Pageant of Words* (Chicago: Scott, Foresman, 1966).

Grimm's Fairy Tales, Selected and Illustrated by Elenore Abbott (New York: Charles Scribner's Sons, 1946).

Melville Bell Grosvenor, ed., *National Geographic Index, 1947–1963* (Washington, D.C.: The National Geographic Society, 1964).

"The Gunniwolf," in Wilhelmina Harper, sel., *Gunniwolf and Other Merry Tales* (Philadelphia: David McKay Company, 1936).

Priscilla Hallowell, *The Long-Nosed Princess, A Fairy Tale* (New York: The Viking Press, 1959).

Mildred Hark and Noel McQueen, *Junior Plays for All Occasions* (Boston: Plays, Inc., 1955).

Wilhelmina Harper, sel., *Gunniwolf and Other Merry Tales* (Philadelphia: David McKay Company, 1936).

Carolyn Haywood, *B Is for Betsy* (New York: Harcourt, Brace & Company, 1939).

Paul Hazard, *Books, Children and Men,* trans. Marguerite Mitchell (Boston: The Horn Book, Inc., 1960).

Robert Hegner, *Parade of the Animal Kingdom* (New York: The Macmillan Company, 1958).

Marguerite Henry, *Born to Trot* (Chicago: Rand McNally & Company, 1950).

Marguerite Henry, *Gaudenzia, Pride of the Palio* (Chicago: Rand McNally & Company, 1960).

Marguerite Henry, *The Little Fellow* (Philadelphia: The John C. Winston Company, 1945).

Marguerite Henry, *Misty of Chincoteague* (Chicago: Rand McNally & Company, 1947).

Kenneth Heuer, *An Adventure in Astronomy* (New York: The Viking Press, 1958).

Thor Heyerdahl, *Kon-tiki, a Special Rand McNally Color Edition for Young People* (Chicago: Rand McNally & Company, 1960).

Du Bose Heyward, *The Country Bunny and the Little Gold Shoes* (Boston: Houghton Mifflin Company, 1939).

Rhoda Hoff, *Why They Wrote* (New York: Henry Z. Walck, Inc., 1961).

Syd Hoff, *Mrs. Switch* (New York: G. P. Putnam's Sons, Inc., 1966).

Melita Hofmann, *The Book of Big Birds* (Garden City, New York: Garden City Books, 1960).

Holling Clancy Holling, *Pagoo* (Boston: Houghton Mifflin Company, 1951).

John Hosier, *The Sorcerer's Apprentice and Other Stories* (New York: Henry Z. Walck, Inc., 1961).

"How the Alphabet Was Made," in Rudyard Kipling, *Just So Stories* (Garden City, New York: Garden City Books, 1952).

Irene Hunt, *Across Five Aprils* (Chicago: Follett Publishing Company, 1964).

Mabel Leigh Hunt, *Better Known as Johnny Appleseed* (Philadelphia: J. B. Lippincott Company, 1950).

Lucia and James L. Hymes, Jr., *Oodles of Noodles* (New York: Young Scott Books, 1964).

Information Please Almanac, Planned and Supervised by Dan Golenpaul Associates (New York: The Macmillan Company).

Keith Gordon Irwin, *The Romance of Writing* (New York: The Viking Press, Inc., 1956).

Joseph Jacobs, sel. and ed., *Indian Fairy Tales* (New York: G. P. Putnam's Sons, n.d.).

Cranston Jones, *Homes of the American Presidents* (New York: McGraw-Hill Book Company, Inc., 1962).

Clara Ingram Judson, *George Washington, Leader of the People* (Chicago: Follett Publishing Company, 1951).

Joseph Nathan Kane, *Famous First Facts* (New York: The H. W. Wilson Company, 1950).

Lee Kingman, ed., *Caldecott Medal Books: 1956–1965* (Boston: Horn Book, Inc., 1965).

Rudyard Kipling, *The Jungle Book* (New York: Grosset & Dunlap, Publishers, 1950).

Rudyard Kipling, *Just So Stories* (Garden City, New York: Garden City Books, 1952).

Daniel C. Knowlton, *Our Beginnings in the Past* (New York: American Book Company, 1933).

Stanley J. Kunitz and Howard Haycraft, eds., *The Junior Book of Authors* (New York: The H. W. Wilson Company, 1951).

R. S. Lambert, *The World's Most Daring Explorers* (New York: Sterling Publishing Co., Inc., 1956).

"The Lambikin," in Joseph Jacobs, sel. and ed., *Indian Fairy Tales* (New York: G. P. Putnam's Sons, n.d.).

Margaret Landon, *Anna and the King of Siam* (New York: The John Day Company, 1944).

Robert Lawson, *Ben and Me* (Boston: Little, Brown and Company, 1951).

Bruce Lee, *Boy's Life of John F. Kennedy* (New York: Sterling Publishing Company, Inc., 1961).

Hellmut Lehmann-Haupt, *The Life of the Book* (New York: Abelard-Schuman, Ltd., 1957).

Lois Lenski, *The Little Auto* (London: Oxford University Press, 1934).

Betty Jean Lifton, *Joji and the Fog* (New York: William Morrow & Company, 1959).

Zada Limerick, ed., *Readers' Guide to Periodical Literature* (New York: The H. W. Wilson Company).

Leo Lionni, *Inch by Inch* (New York: Ivan Obolonsky, Inc., 1960).

"Little Cabin in the Woods," words by Betty Welsbacher, in Eunice Boardman and Beth Landis, *Exploring Music 1* (New York: Holt, Rinehart and Winston, 1966).

Hugh Lofting, *Dr. Dolittle's Post Office* (Philadelphia: J. B. Lippincott Company, 1951).

Jack London, *The Call of the Wild* (New York: The Macmillan Company, 1958).

E. L. McAdams, Jr. and George Milne, *Johnson's Dictionary, A Modern Selection* (New York: Pantheon Books, 1963).

Adeline McCall, *Timothy's Tunes* (Boston Music Company, 1943).

Marshall McClintock, *Here Is a Book* (New York: The Vanguard Press, 1939).

Robert McCloskey, *Blueberries for Sal* (New York: The Viking Press, 1948).

Robert McCloskey, *Homer Price* (New York: The Viking Press, 1949).

Betty McDonald, *Mrs. Piggle-Wiggle* (Philadelphia: J. B. Lippincott Company, 1947).

Gladys Malvern, *Dancing Star: The Story of Anna Pavlova* (New York: Julian Messner Inc., 1942).

Thalia Mara, *First Steps in Ballet* (Garden City, New York: Garden City Books, 1955).

George F. Mason, *Animal Tails* (New York: William Morrow and Company, 1958).

George F. Mason, *Animal Weapons* (New York: William Morrow and Company, 1949).

Enid L. Meadowcroft, *The Gift of the River* (New York: Thomas Y. Crowell Company, 1937).

Cornelia Meigs, *Wind in the Chimney* (New York: The Macmillan Company, 1958).

Bertha M. Miller and Elinor W. Fields, eds., *Caldecott Medal Books: 1938–1957* (Boston: Horn Book, Inc., 1957).

Bertha M. Miller and Elinor W. Field, eds., *Caldecott Medal Books: 1922–1955* (Boston: Horn Book, Inc., 1955).

Olive Beaupré Miller, ed., *My Book House* (Chicago: Book House for Children, 1950).

Olive Beaupré Miller, *Picturesque Tale of Progress* (Chicago: Book House for Children, 1949).

Ralph Moody, *Little Britches* (New York: W. W. Norton & Company, 1950).

Montrose J. Moses, ed., *A Treasury of Plays for Children* (Boston: Little, Brown and Company, 1921).

Jeannette Covert Nolan, *Queen Elizabeth* (Evanston, Illinois: Row, Peterson and Company, 1951).

Ruth Nordlie, *A Dog for Susie* (Chicago: Children's Press, Inc., 1960).

Andre Norton, *Catseye* (New York: Harcourt, Brace & World, Inc., 1961).

Robert O'Brien and the Editors of *Life, Machines* (New York: Time Incorporated, 1964).

"Off the Shelf," in Mildred Hark and Noel McQueen, *Junior Plays for All Occasions* (Boston: Plays, Inc., 1955).

Oscar Ogg, *The 26 Letters* (New York: Thomas Y. Crowell Company, 1961).

Once Upon a Word (Chicago: Scott, Foresman, 1966).

Mary O'Neill, *Hailstones and Halibut Bones, Adventures in Color* (Garden City, New York: Doubleday & Company, Inc., 1961).

Edward Osmond, *From Drumbeat to Tickertape* (New York: Criterion Books, Inc., 1960).

Tony Palazzo, *A Dinosaur Alphabet* (New York: Duell, Sloan & Pearce, Inc., 1963).

Bill Peet, *Huge Harold* (Boston: Houghton Mifflin Company, 1961).

Beatrix Potter, *The Tale of Peter Rabbit* (New York: Frederick Warne & Co., Inc., n.d.).

Isabel Proudfit, *The Treasure Hunter* (N.Y.: Julian Messner, 1939).

The Real Mother Goose (Chicago: Rand McNally & Co., 1916).

H. A. Rey, *Curious George* (Boston: Houghton Mifflin Company, 1941).

H. A. Rey, *Know the Stars* (Boston: Houghton Mifflin Company, 1954).

William Wilcox Robinson, *Beasts of the Tar Pits,* rev. ed. (Los Angeles, California: The Ward Ritchie Press, 1961).

Frances Rogers, *Painted Rock to Printed Page* (Philadelphia: J. B. Lippincott Company, 1950).

Sidney Rosen, *Galileo and the Magic Numbers* (Boston: Little, Brown and Company, 1958).

Elizabeth Rubin, *The Curies and Radium* (New York: Franklin Watts, Inc., 1961).

Eloise Rue, comp., *Subject Index to Books for Intermediate Grades* (Chicago: American Library Association, 1950).

Julia L. Sauer, *Mike's House* (New York: The Viking Press, 1954).

John M. Schealer, *This Way to the Stars* (New York: E. P. Dutton & Company, 1957).

William Earl Scheele, *Prehistoric Animals* (Cleveland: The World Publishing Company, 1954).

Margaret C. Scoggin, comp., *Escapes and Rescues* (New York: Alfred A. Knopf, Inc., 1960).

"Scrapefoot," in Kate Douglas Wiggin and Nora Archibald Smith, *Tales of Laughter* (Garden City, New York: Doubleday & Company, Inc., 1908).

Ruth Crawford Seeger, *American Folk Songs for Children in Home, School and Nursery School* (Garden City, New York: Doubleday & Company, Inc., 1948).

Catherine F. Sellew, *Adventures with the Gods* (Boston: Little, Brown and Company, 1945).

Dr. Seuss, *The 500 Hats of Bartholomew Cubbins* (New York: The Vanguard Press, 1938).

George Earlie Shankle, *State Names, Flags, Seals, Songs, Birds, Flowers, and Other Symbols,* rev. ed. (New York: The H. W. Wilson Company, 1941).

Philip M. Sherlock, *Anansi the Spider Man* (New York: Thomas Y. Crowell Company, 1954).

"Shingebiss," in Olive Beaupré Miller, ed., *My Book House, Vol. II: Story Time* (Chicago: Book House for Children, 1950).

Katherine B. Shippen, *Mr. Bell Invents the Telephone* (New York: Random House, Inc., 1952).

Skadsheim Topical Index to the National Geographic Magazine (Angwin, California: Angwin Book Bindery, 1964).

Esphyr Slobodkina, *Caps for Sale* (New York: William R. Scott, Inc., 1947).

Irene Smith, *A History of the Newbery and Caldecott Medals* (New York: The Viking Press, 1957).

Edmund Spenser, *Saint George and the Dragon,* adapted by S. S. Warburg (Boston: Houghton Mifflin Company, 1963).

Armstrong Sperry, *Voyages of Christopher Columbus* (New York: Random House, Inc., 1950).

Claus Stamm, *Three Strong Women* (New York: The Viking Press, 1962).

Evelyn Stefansson, *Within the Circle* (New York: Charles Scribner's Sons, 1945).

Augusta Stevenson, *Virginia Dare, Mystery Girl* (New York: The Bobbs-Merrill Company, Inc., 1958).

Robert Louis Stevenson, *Treasure Island* (New York: Grosset & Dunlap, Publishers, 1947).

The Story of the Three Little Pigs with drawings by Leslie Brooke (New York: Frederick Warne & Company Ltd., n.d.).

Subcommittee of the American Library Association Editorial Committee, comp., *Subject and Title Index to Short Stories for Children* (Chicago: American Library Association, 1955).

Ronald Syme, *Vasco da Gama, Sailor Toward the Sunrise* (New York: William Morrow & Company, 1959).

Harlan Tarbell, *The Chalk Talk Manual* (Minneapolis: T. S. Denison & Company, Inc., 1962).

"The Three Billy Goats Gruff," in P. C. Asbjønsen and J. E. Moe, *East O' the Sun and West O' the Moon* (Garden City, New York: Junior DeLuxe Edition, 1957).

Henry Thomas, *Copernicus* (New York: Julian Messner, Inc., 1960).

"The Tiger, The Brahman, and the Jackal," in Joseph Jacobs, sel. and ed., *Indian Fairy Tales* (New York: G. P. Putnam's Sons, n.d.).

"Travels of a Fox," in May Hill Arbuthnot, comp., *Time for Fairy Tales, Old and New* (Chicago: Scott, Foresman and Company, 1952).

P. L. Travers, *Mary Poppins* (New York: Harcourt, Brace & Company, 1934).

Mark Twain, *The Adventures of Tom Sawyer* (New York: Grosset & Dunlap, Publishers, 1946).

Yoshiko Uchida, *The Dancing Kettle* (New York: Harcourt, Brace & Company, 1949).

United Nations Educational, Scientific, and Cultural Organization, comp., *700 Science Experiments for Everyone* (Garden City, New York: Doubleday & Company, Inc., 1958).

Hilda van Stockum, *The Cottage at Bantry Bay* (New York: The Viking Press, Inc., 1938).

Jean Brown Wagoner, *Jane Addams, Little Lame Girl* (New York: The Bobbs-Merrill Company, 1944).

Leslie Waller, *A Book to Begin On, Our American Language* (New York: Holt, Rinehart and Winston, 1960).

Ruth Cromer Weir, *John Paul Jones* (Evanston, Illinois: Row, Peterson and Company, 1950).

Jane Werner, ed., *The Golden Book of Poetry* (New York: Simon & Schuster, 1949).

Dorothy Herbert West and Rachel Shor, eds., *Children's Catalog* (New York: The H. W. Wilson Company, 1961).

What Goes into a Dictionary (Chicago: Scott, Foresman, 1965).

E. B. White, *Charlotte's Web* (New York: Harper & Brothers, Publishers, 1952).

Kate Douglas Wiggin and Nora Archibald Smith, eds., *Tales of Laughter* (Garden City, New York: Doubleday & Company, Inc., 1908).

Margaret Williamson, *First Book of Bugs* (New York: Franklin Watts, Inc., 1949).

Irving Wolfe, Beatrice Perhame Krone, Margaret Fullerton, *Music Across the Country* (Chicago: Follett Publishing Company, 1956).

The World Almanac and Book of Facts, ed. by Luman H. Long (New York: Newspaper Enterprise Association).

Lee Wyndham, *Dancers, Dancers, Dancers* (New York: Franklin Watts, Inc., 1961).

George J. Zaffo, *The Big Book of Real Trains* (New York: Grosset & Dunlap, Inc., 1949).

Herbert Zim, *The Great Whales* (New York: William Morrow & Company, 1951).

Appendix II

THE CALDECOTT MEDAL BOOKS

1968 Barbara Emberley, adapter, *Drummer Hoff* (New Jersey: Prentice-Hall, 1967).

1967 Evaline Ness, *Sam, Bangs and Moonshine* (New York: Holt, Rinehart and Winston, Inc., 1966).

1966 Sorche Nic Leodhas, *Always Room for One More* (New York: Holt, Rinehart and Winston, 1965).

1965 Beatrice Schenk De Regniers, *May I Bring a Friend?* (New York: Atheneum Publishers, 1964).

1964 Maurice Sendak, *Where the Wild Things Are* (New York: Harper & Row, 1963).

1963 Ezra Jack Keats, *The Snowy Day* (New York: The Viking Company, 1962).

1962 Marcia Brown, *Once a Mouse* (New York: Charles Scribner's Sons, 1961).

1961 Ruth Robbins, *Baboushka and the Three Kings* (Berkeley, California: Parnassus Press, 1960).

1960 Marie Ets and Aurora Labastida, *Nine Days to Christmas* (New York: The Viking Press, 1959).

1959 Barbara Cooney, *Chanticleer and the Fox,* adapted (New York: Thomas Y. Crowell Company, 1958).

1958 Robert McCloskey, *Time of Wonder* (New York: The Viking Press, 1957).

1957 Janice May Udry, *A Tree Is Nice* (New York: Harper & Brothers, Publishers, 1956).

1956 John Langstaff, *Frog Went A-Courtin'* retold (New York: Harcourt, Brace & Company, 1955).

1955 Marcia Brown, *Cinderella, A Free Translation from the French of Charles Perrault* (New York: Charles Scribner's Sons, 1954).

1954 Ludwig Bemelmans, *Madeline's Rescue* (New York: The Viking Press, 1953).

1953 Lynd Ward, *The Biggest Bear* (Boston: Houghton Mifflin Company, 1952).

1952 Will and Nicolas, *Finders Keepers* (New York: Harcourt, Brace & Company, 1951).

1951 Katherine Milhous, *The Egg Tree* (New York: Charles Scribner's Sons, 1950).

1950 Leo Politi, *Song of the Swallows* (New York: Charles Scribner's Sons, 1949).

1949 Berta and Elmer Hader, *The Big Snow* (New York: The Macmillan Company, 1948).

1948 Alvin Tresselt, *White Snow, Bright Snow* (New York: Lothrop, Lee and Shepard Company, Inc., 1947).

1947 Golden McDonald, *The Little Island* (New York: Doubleday & Company, Inc., 1946).

1946 Maud and Miska Petersham, *The Rooster Crows* (New York: The Macmillan Company, 1945).

1945 Rachel Field, *Prayer for a Child* (New York: The Macmillan Company, 1944).

1944 James Thurber, *Many Moons* (New York: Harcourt, Brace & Company, 1943).

1943 Virginia Lee Burton, *The Little House* (Boston: Houghton Mifflin Company, 1942).

1942 Robert McCloskey, *Make Way for Ducklings* (New York: The Viking Press, 1941).

1941 Robert Lawson, *They Were Strong and Good* (New York: The Viking Press, 1940).

1940 Ingri & Edgar Parin d'Aulaire, *Abraham Lincoln* (New York: Doubleday & Company, Inc., 1939).

1939 Thomas Handforth, *Mei Li* (New York: Doubleday & Company, Inc., 1938).

1938 Helen Dean Fish, *Animals of the Bible, from the King James' Bible*. Illustrated by Dorothy P. Lathrop with text by Helen Dean Fish (Philadelphia: J. B. Lippincott Company, 1937).

THE NEWBERY MEDAL BOOKS

1968 Elaine L. Konigsburg, *From the Mixed-up Files of Mrs. Basil E. Frankweiler* (New York: Atheneum, 1967).

1967 Irene Hunt, *Up a Road Slowly* (Chicago: Follett Publishing Company, 1966).

1966 Elizabeth Borton de Treviño, *I, Juan de Pareja* (New York: Farrar, Straus & Giroux, 1965).

1965 Maia Wojciechowska, *Shadow of a Bull* (New York: Atheneum Publishers, 1964).

1964 Emily C. Neville, *It's Like This Cat* (New York: Harper & Row, 1963).

1963 Madeleine L'Engle, *A Wrinkle in Time* (New York: Farrar, Straus and Company, 1962).

1962 Elizabeth George Speare, *The Bronze Bow* (Boston: Houghton Mifflin Company, 1961).

1961 Scott O'Dell, *The Island of the Blue Dolphins* (Boston: Houghton Mifflin Company, 1960).

1960 Joseph Krumgold, *Onion John* (New York: Thomas Y. Crowell Company, 1959).

1959 Elizabeth George Speare, *The Witch of Blackbird Pond* (Boston: Houghton Mifflin Company, 1958).

1958 Harold Keith, *Rifles for Watie* (New York: Thomas Y. Crowell Company, 1957).

1957 Virginia E. Sorenson, *Miracles on Maple Hill* (New York: Harcourt, Brace & Company, 1956).

1956 Jean Lee Latham, *Carry On, Mr. Bowditch* (Boston: Houghton Mifflin Company, 1955).

1955 Meindert De Jong, *The Wheel on the School* (New York: Harper & Brothers, Publishers, 1954).

1954 Joseph Krumgold, *And Now Miguel* (New York: Thomas Y. Crowell Company, 1953).

1953 Ann Nolan Clark, *Secret of the Andes* (New York: The Viking Press, 1952).

1952 Eleanor Estes, *Ginger Pye* (New York: Harcourt, Brace & Company, 1951).

1951 Elizabeth Yates, *Amos Fortune, Free Man* (New York: E. P. Dutton & Co., Inc., 1950).

1950 Marguerite de Angeli, *The Door in the Wall* (Garden City, New York: Doubleday & Company, Inc., 1949).

1949 Marguerite Henry, *King of the Wind* (New York: Rand McNally & Company, 1948).

1948 William Pené du Bois, *The Twenty-One Balloons* (New York: The Viking Press, 1947).

1947 Carolyn Sherwin Bailey, *Miss Hickory* (New York: The Viking Press, 1946).

1946 Lois Lenski, *Strawberry Girl* (Philadelphia: J. B. Lippincott Company, 1945).

1945 Robert Lawson, *Rabbit Hill* (New York: The Viking Press, 1944).

1944 Esther Forbes, *Johnny Tremain* (Boston: Houghton Mifflin Company, 1943).

1943 Elizabeth Janet Gray, *Adam of the Road* (New York: The Viking Press, 1942).

1942 Walter D. Edmonds, *The Matchlock Gun* (New York: Dodd, Mead & Company, 1941).

1941 Armstrong Sperry, *Call It Courage* (New York: The Macmillan Company, 1940).

1940 James Daugherty, *Daniel Boone* (New York: The Viking Press, 1939).

1939 Elizabeth Enright, *Thimble Summer* (New York: Rinehart & Company Incorporated, 1938).

1938 Kate Seredy, *The White Stag* (New York: The Viking Press, 1937).

1937 Ruth Sawyer, *Roller Skates* (New York: The Viking Press, 1936).

1936 Carol Ryrie Brink, *Caddie Woodlawn* (New York: The Macmillan Company, 1935).

1935 Monica Shannon, *Dobry* (New York: The Viking Company, 1934).

1934 Cornelia Meigs, *Invincible Louisa* (Boston: Little, Brown and Company, 1933).

1933 Elizabeth Foreman Lewis, *Young Fu of the Upper Yangtze* (Philadelphia: The John Winston Company, 1932).

1932 Laura Adams Armer, *Waterless Mountain* (New York: Longmans, Green and Co., 1931).

1931 Elizabeth Coatsworth, *The Cat Who Went to Heaven* (New York: The Macmillan Company, 1930).

1930 Rachel Field, *Hitty, Her First Hundred Years* (New York: The Macmillan Company, 1929).

1929 Eric P. Kelly, *Trumpeter of Krakow* (New York: The Macmillan Company, 1928).

1928 Dhan Gopal Mukerji, *Gay-Neck, The Story of a Pigeon* (New York: E. P. Dutton & Co., Inc., 1927).

1927 Will James, *Smoky, the Cowhorse* (New York: Charles Scribner's Sons, 1926).

1926 Arthur Bowie Chrisman, *Shen of the Sea* (New York: E. P. Dutton & Co., Inc., 1925).

1925 Charles Finger, *Tales from Silver Lands* (Garden City, New York: Doubleday & Company, Inc., 1924).

1924 Charles Boardman Hawes, *The Dark Frigate* (Boston: Little, Brown and Company, 1923).

1923 Hugh Lofting, *The Voyages of Doctor Dolittle* (Philadelphia: J. B. Lippincott Company, 1922).

1922 Hendrik Willem Van Loon, *The Story of Mankind* (New York: Liveright Publishing Corp., 1921).

Appendix III

Reference Materials Cited in

the Text

ATLASES

American History Atlas (Maplewood, New Jersey: C. S. Hammond & Company, 1963).

Harry S. Ashmore, ed., *Encyclopaedia Britannica World Atlas* (Chicago: William Benton, Publisher; Encyclopaedia Britannica, Inc., 1961).

Frank Debenham, *The Global Atlas* (New York: Simon & Schuster, Inc., Publishers, 1958).

Edward B. Espenshade, Jr., *Goode's World Atlas* (Chicago: Rand McNally & Company, 1964).

Hammond's Advanced Reference Atlas (New York: C. S. Hammond & Company, Inc., 1949).

Hammond's Historical Atlas (Maplewood, New Jersey: C. S. Hammond & Company, Inc., 1960).

Hammond's Standard World Atlas (Maplewood, New Jersey: C. S. Hammond & Company, Inc., 1958).

E. L. Jordan, *Hammond's Nature Atlas of America* (Maplewood, New Jersey: C. S. Hammond & Company, Inc., 1952).

Clifford L. and Elizabeth H. Lord, *Historical Atlas of the United States*, rev. ed. (New York: Henry Holt and Company, 1953).

AUDIO-VISUAL MATERIALS

The authors recommend that any librarian wishing a list of audio-visual materials for use in the teaching of library skills secure a copy of *Instructional Materials for Teaching the Use of the Library* by Shirley L. Hopkinson, Ed.D., Associate Professor, San Jose State College, San Jose, California. Published by Claremont House, 1967. This booklet may be secured from Dr. Hopkinson for $1.10 by writing her at the Department of Education, San Jose State College, San Jose, California.

Records

Babes in Toyland. Golden. 78AB. 33⅓ rpm.

The Flea, et al. Ruth Sawyer, Storyteller. Weston Woods Studios. 701, 702.

The Frog. A Spanish Folk Tale. Told by Ruth Sawyer. Presented by the American Library Association. RCA. D8–CC–224–225. 78rpm.

Sorcerer's Apprentice. RCA Victor. LM 2056. 33⅓ rpm.

Music Stories. "The Firebird." Igor Stravinsky. F8–Sp–6759–6760. (14:58 minutes). Microgroove. 33⅓ rpm. RCA Victor Record Division. The Jam Handy Organization.

                        accompanied by filmstrip

. . . Film 5. Edward Kozak and Frances Boddy. Illustrated by Eko. The Jam Handy Organization, 2821 S. Grand Blvd., Detroit, Michigan, ©1953.

Filmstrips

THE FIREBIRD. See *Music Stories* above.

STORIES BEHIND WORDS. Curriculum Films, 1951. 3rd ed., 18th printing. 29fr. color (Language Arts Series).

Films

. . . AND NOW MIGUEL. Joseph Krumgold for U.S.I.A., 1953. 63 min. b&w.

THE DOUGHNUTS. Based on Robert McCloskey's *Homer Price.* Weston Woods. 26 min. b&w/color.

HEIDI. Teaching Film Custodians, Inc. 38 min. b&w.

JOHNNY APPLESEED: A LEGEND OF FRONTIER LIFE. Coronet Films. 13 min. b&w/color. Two other films on Johnny Appleseed are also available. One is produced by Disney, the other by High School Reading Films.

THE STEADFAST TIN SOLDIER. Danish Culture Film, 1955. 14 min. color.

THE STORY OF A BOOK. Churchill Films. 11 min. b&w/color.

TREASURE ISLAND. MGM, edited by Teaching Film Custodians, Inc. 43 min. b&w.

THE UGLY DUCKLING. Encyclopaedia Britannica Educational Corporation. 11 min. b&w/color. Another film of *The Ugly Duckling* is produced by Coronet Films.

DICTIONARIES

E. Cobham Brewer, *Brewer's Dictionary of Phrase and Fable* (New York: Harper & Row, 1963) .

Stuart A. Courtis, et al, *The Courtis-Watters Illustrated Golden Dictionary for Young Readers* (New York: Simon and Schuster, Inc., Publishers, n.d.) .

P. D. Eastman, *The Cat in the Hat Beginner Book Dictionary* (New York: Random House, Inc., 1964) .

Isaac K. Funk, ed., *Funk and Wagnalls New "Standard" Dictionary of the English Language* (New York: Funk & Wagnalls Company, 1961) .

Funk & Wagnalls Standard Dictionary of the English Language International Edition Combined with Britannica World Language Dictionary, 2 vols. (Chicago: Encyclopaedia Britannica, Inc., 1960) .

Philip Babcock Gove, ed., *Webster's Third New International Dictionary of the English Language Unabridged* (Springfield, Massachusetts: G. & C. Merriam Company, Publishers, 1961) .

Dilla W. MacBean, *Picture Book Dictionary with a Picture Story* (Chicago: Children's Press, Inc., 1952) .

G. & C. Merriam, *Webster's Elementary Dictionary for Boys and Girls* (Springfield, Massachusetts: Merriam Company, n.d.) .

G. & C. Merriam, *Webster's New Practical School Dictionary* (Springfield, Massachusetts: Merriam Co., 1964) .

G. & C. Merriam, *Webster's Seventh New Collegiate Dictionary* (Springfield, Massachusetts: Merriam Co., 1963) .

E. L. Thorndike and Clarence L. Barnhart, *Thorndike & Barnhart Beginning Dictionary* (Chicago: Scott, Foresman and Company, n.d.) .

E. L. Thorndike and Clarence L. Barnhart, *Thorndike-Barnhart Junior Dictionary* (Chicago: Scott, Foresman and Company, n.d.) .

Ellen Wales Walpole, *The Golden Dictionary* (New York: Simon and Schuster, Inc., Publishers, 1944) .

Webster's Biographical Dictionary (Springfield, Massachusetts: G. & C. Merriam Co., Publishers, 1956) .

Webster's New World Dictionary—Elementary Edition (New York: American Book Company, 1961) .

Webster's Geographical Dictionary (Springfield, Massachusetts: G. & C. Merriam Co., Publishers, 1955).

Wendell W. Wright, *The Rainbow Dictionary* (Cleveland: The World Publishing Company, 1947).

Young People's Science Dictionary by the editors of the *Young People's Science Encyclopedia* (Chicago: Children's Press, Inc., 1964).

ENCYCLOPEDIAS

Dorothy A. Bennett, *Golden Encyclopedia* (New York: Simon and Schuster, Inc., Publishers, 1946).

The Book of Popular Science (New York: Grolier Incorporated).

Britannica Book of the Year (Chicago: William Benton, Publisher; Encyclopaedia Britannica, Inc.).

Britannica Junior Encyclopaedia for Boys and Girls (Chicago: Encyclopaedia Britannica, Inc.).

Compton's Pictured Encyclopedia and Fact-Index (Chicago: F. E. Compton Company; Division of Encyclopaedia Britannica, Inc.).

Compton's Yearbook (Chicago: F. E. Compton & Company).

The Lincoln Library of Essential Information, 2 vols. (Buffalo, New York: The Frontier Press).

Richard B. Morris, ed., *Encyclopedia of American History* (New York: Harper & Row, 1961).

National College of Education, Evanston, Illinois, eds., *Young People's Science Encyclopedia* (Chicago: Children's Press, Inc.).

Bertha Morris Parker, *Golden Book Encyclopedia,* 16 vols. (New York: Golden Press, 1959).

The World Book Encyclopedia (Chicago: Field Enterprises Educational Corporation).

The World Book Year Book. The Annual Supplement to the World Book Encyclopedia (Chicago: Field Enterprises Educational Corporation, Publishers).

Herbert S. Zim, ed., et al, *Our Wonderful World, An Encyclopedic Anthology for the Entire Family* (Chicago: Spencer Press, Inc.).

PERIODICALS

The Booklist and Subscription Books Bulletin (Chicago: American Library Association).

The Golden Magazine for Boys and Girls (Poughkeepsie, New York: Golden Press, Inc.).

Highlights for Children (Honesdale, Pennsylvania: Highlights for Children, Inc.).

The Horn Book Magazine (Boston: The Horn Book, Incorporated).

Jack and Jill (Philadelphia: The Curtis Publishing Company).

Model Airplane News (New York: Air Age, Inc.).

National Geographic (Washington, D.C.: National Geographic Society).

Road and Track (Newport Beach, California: Bond Publishing Co.).

Glossary of Terms

Accession number: The number assigned to a book to provide a numerical count of the total number of books entering a collection.

Almanac: A book containing a calendar and statistics about persons, places, and things.

Analytic card: A card in the card catalog that resembles a subject card but refers to the pages covering the specific subject.

Anthology: A book containing a collection of short stories, poems, or some other form of literature.

Appendix: A section at the end of a book containing supporting materials.

Atlas: A collection of maps.

Audio-visuals: A term used to indicate records, transparencies, film-strips, etc., and the machines used to operate them.

Author card: A catalog card with the name of the author on the top line.

Bibliography: A list of books or other writings on a particular subject.

Biography: The written history of a person's life.

Book card: The card used to represent the book borrowed from the library.

Book pocket: A paper pocket pasted in the inside cover to hold the book card.

Call number: The classification number and Cutter-Sanborn letter and number which identify the book by subject and author.

Card catalog: The index to all the books in the library.

Cataloging: The process of assigning call numbers to books so that all like subject matter will be grouped together.

Charging desk: The place where the user has his books charged out or in.

Classification number: The number assigned to a book by its subject.

Concentrated program: Instruction in library skills given several times a week for a portion of the school year.

Copyright: The exclusive right to reproduce, publish, and sell literary or artistic works.

Cross reference: A catalog card directing the user to another heading. The *see* reference directs one to another entry for information; the *see also* indicates additional entries.

Cutter-Sanborn number: A combination of characters representing an author's surname, composed of an initial letter or the first letters followed by numbers to make the numerical order of the symbols correspond to the alphabetical order of the names.

Dewey Decimal Classification System: A system of dividing nonfiction books into ten major classes by subject matter, with further subdivision in each class.

Dictionary: A reference in which the words of any language are entered alphabetically and defined.

Easy books: Books whose contents appeal particularly to young children.

Encyclopedia: A book or set of books containing information on all subjects or covering major points of one subject.

Entry: A name, word, or phrase used as a heading.

Fiction: Imagined or created stories.

Flannelboard: A surface covered with flannel to which specially backed materials adhere; used for instruction or other purposes.

Gazetteer: A geographical dictionary.

Glossary: A listing of definitions of special terms in a book.

Guide words: Words or phrases at the top of a page to facilitate the locating of a particular word or topic.

Illustrator: The artist who creates the drawings or paintings in a book.

Index: An alphabetical list of subjects in a given book, giving references to pages containing information on each subject.

Large-group instruction: All sections of a grade level receive instruction as one group.

Multi-media: A term used to indicate various means of communication.

Non-fiction: A book presenting true information.

Opaque projector: A machine that enlarges by projection flat or semi-flat, opaque material.

Overhead projector: A machine using a variety of transparent materials and devices whose use enables the instructor to face the class.

Periodical: A magazine or newspaper.

Publisher: A person or company responsible for producing printed materials.

Reference book: A book containing factual information about people, places, and things.

Signature: A printed sheet containing a number of pages folded as one unit and forming a section of a book.

Spine: The backbone of a book.

Subject card: A catalog card with the subject on the top line.

Subject heading: The word or words used to indicate the subject of the book.

Table of contents: A list in the front of a book giving the sections the book contains, in the order of their appearance in the book.

Tipping pages: The process of inserting a loose page into its correct place in the book. This is done by running a thin stream of glue along the inside edge of the page.

Title card: A catalog card with the title on the top line.

Transparency: Matter printed on transparent material to be enlarged by overhead projection.

Vertical file: A cabinet of drawers containing pictures and pamphlets.

Year book: A volume that is issued yearly in order to give up-to-date information.

Index